The Latest Ninja Dual Air Fryer Cookbook 2025

2000 Days Tasty and Affordable Ninja Air Fryer Recipes for Beginners to Cook Faster and Healthier

Leanne J. Hays

All Rights Reserved.

The contents of this book may not be reproduced, copied or transmitted without the direct written permission of the author or publisher. Under no circumstances will the publisher or the author be held responsible or liable for any damage, compensation or pecuniary loss arising directly or indirectly from the information contained in this book.

Legal notice. This book is protected by copyright. It is intended for personal use only. You may not modify, distribute, sell, use, quote or paraphrase any part or content of this book without the consent of the author or publisher.

Notice Of Disclaimer.

Please note that the information in this document is intended for educational and entertainment purposes only. Every effort has been made to provide accurate, up-to-date, reliable and complete information. No warranty of any kind is declared or implied. The reader acknowledges that the author does not engage in the provision of legal, financial, medical or professional advice. The content in this book has been obtained from a variety of sources. Please consult a licensed professional before attempting any of the techniques described in this book. By reading this document, the reader agrees that in no event shall the author be liable for any direct or indirect damages, including but not limited to errors, omissions or inaccuracies, resulting from the use of the information in this document.

CONTENTS

Breakfast Recipes 12

Spinach Egg Muffins 12

Cinnamon Apple French Toast 12

Nutty Granola 12

Cinnamon Toasts 13

Sausage & Bacon Omelet 13

Wholemeal Banana-walnut Bread 13

Egg In Bread Hole 14

Mozzarella Bacon Calzones 14

Egg White Muffins 14

Sausage And Cheese Balls 15

Pepper Egg Cups 15

Sausage And Egg Breakfast Burrito 15

Breakfast Sausage Omelet 16

Honey Banana Oatmeal 16

Egg And Avocado In The Ninja Foodi 16

Sausage & Butternut Squash 17

Bacon Cheese Egg With Avocado And Potato Nuggets 17

Eggs In Avocado Cups 17

Gyro Breakfast Patties With Tzatziki 18

Easy Pancake Doughnuts 18

Air Fryer Sausage Patties 18

Yellow Potatoes With Eggs 19

Wholemeal Blueberry Muffins 19

Cinnamon Rolls 19

Banana Bread 20

Quiche Breakfast Peppers 20

Egg And Bacon Muffins ... 20
Baked Mushroom And Mozzarella Frittata With Breakfast Potatoes ... 21
Vanilla Strawberry Doughnuts ... 21
Donuts ... 22
Cinnamon-raisin Bagels Everything Bagels ... 22
Canadian Bacon Muffin Sandwiches And All-in-one Toast ... 23
Breakfast Potatoes ... 23
Asparagus And Bell Pepper Strata And Greek Bagels ... 24
Morning Patties ... 24
Puff Pastry ... 25
Cinnamon Air Fryer Apples ... 25
Parmesan Ranch Risotto And Oat And Chia Porridge ... 25
Breakfast Meatballs ... 26
Breakfast Stuffed Peppers ... 26
Pumpkin French Toast Casserole With Sweet And Spicy Twisted Bacon ... 26

Fish And Seafood Recipes ... 27

Chili Honey Salmon ... 27
Fried Prawns ... 27
Tuna-stuffed Quinoa Patties ... 27
Bang Bang Shrimp With Roasted Bok Choy ... 28
Bacon-wrapped Shrimp ... 28
Miso Salmon And Oyster Po'boy ... 29
Honey Pecan Shrimp ... 29
Basil Cheese Salmon ... 30
Keto Baked Salmon With Pesto ... 30
Rainbow Salmon Kebabs And Tuna Melt ... 30
Parmesan-crusted Fish Sticks With Baked Macaroni And Cheese ... 31
Two-way Salmon ... 31
Cod With Jalapeño ... 32

Prawn Creole Casserole And Garlic Lemon Scallops	32
Butter-wine Baked Salmon	32
Basil Cheese S·saltalmon	33
Fried Lobster Tails	33
Orange-mustard Glazed Salmon	33
Thai Prawn Skewers And Lemon-tarragon Fish En Papillote	34
Lemon Pepper Fish Fillets	34
Perfect Parmesan Salmon	35
Tandocri Prawns	35
Dukkah-crusted Halibut	35
Savory Salmon Fillets	36
Fried Tilapia	36
Panko-crusted Fish Sticks	36
Broiled Crab Cakes With Hush Puppies	37
Classic Fish Sticks With Tartar Sauce	37
Frozen Breaded Fish Fillet	38
Crustless Prawn Quiche	38
Roasted Salmon Fillets & Chilli Lime Prawns	38
Blackened Red Snapper	39
Herbed Prawns Pita	39
Steamed Cod With Garlic And Swiss Chard	39
Country Prawns	40
Tuna With Herbs	40
Salmon With Broccoli And Cheese	40
Nutty Prawns With Amaretto Glaze	41
Stuffed Mushrooms With Crab	41
Marinated Salmon Fillets	41
Fish Sandwich	42

Beef, Pork, And Lamb Recipes 42

Steak And Asparagus Bundles 42

Sausage And Cauliflower Arancini 43

Jerk-rubbed Pork Loin With Carrots And Sage 43

Sumptuous Pizza Tortilla Rolls 44

Bbq Pork Chops 44

Meat And Rice Stuffed Peppers 44

Cheeseburgers With Barbecue Potato Chips 45

Garlic Butter Steaks 45

Pork Chops With Apples 46

Glazed Steak Recipe 46

Five-spice Pork Belly 46

Roast Beef With Yorkshire Pudding 47

New York Strip Steak 47

Kielbasa Sausage With Pineapple And Kheema Meatloaf 48

Asian Pork Skewers 48

Steak In Air Fry 49

Turkey And Beef Meatballs 49

Easy Breaded Pork Chops 49

Mongolian Beef With Sweet Chili Brussels Sprouts 50

Garlic Butter Steak Bites 50

Spicy Lamb Chops 51

Barbecue Ribs With Roasted Green Beans And Shallots 51

Meatballs 51

Ham Burger Patties 52

Taco Seasoned Steak 52

Sweet And Spicy Country-style Ribs 52

Bacon Wrapped Pork Tenderloin 53

Roasted Beef 53

Meatloaf 53

Rosemary And Garlic Lamb Chops 54

Rosemary Ribeye Steaks And Mongolian-style Beef 54

Chinese Bbq Pork 55

Gochujang Brisket 55

Lamb Shank With Mushroom Sauce 56

Tomahawk Steak 56

Beef Kofta Kebab 57

Beef Rbs Ii 57

Bacon-wrapped Filet Mignon 57

Cinnamon-apple Pork Chops 58

Yogurt Lamb Chops 58

Bbq Pork Spare Ribs 58

Poultry Recipes 59

Simply Terrific Turkey Meatballs 59

Honey Butter Chicken 59

Chicken Bites 59

Chicken And Vegetable Fajitas 60

Air-fried Turkey Breast With Roasted Green Bean Casserole 60

Greek Chicken Souvlaki 61

Bacon-wrapped Chicken 61

Chipotle Drumsticks 61

Greek Chicken Meatballs 62

Honey-glazed Chicken Thighs 62

Chicken And Potatoes 62

Cornish Hen With Asparagus 63

Chicken Thighs In Waffles 63

Wings With Corn On The Cob 64

Sesame Ginger Chicken 64

Balsamic Duck Breast 64

Whole Chicken 65

Fajita Chicken Strips & Barbecued Chicken With Creamy Coleslaw 65

Crispy Dill Chicken Strips 66

Almond Chicken 66

Chicken Breast Strips 66

Glazed Thighs With French Fries 67

Roasted Garlic Chicken Pizza With Cauliflower "wings" 67

Crusted Chicken Breast 68

"fried" Chicken With Warm Baked Potato Salad 68

Brazilian Chicken Drumsticks 69

Lemon-pepper Chicken Thighs With Buttery Roasted Radishes 69

Chicken Parmesan 70

Bang-bang Chicken 70

Cheddar-stuffed Chicken 70

Chicken Patties And One-dish Chicken Rice 71

Chicken Shawarma 71

Curried Orange Honey Chicken 72

Spicy Chicken 72

Chicken & Veggies 72

Teriyaki Chicken Skewers 73

Pecan-crusted Chicken Tenders 73

Cornish Hen 73

Spicy Chicken Sandwiches With "fried" Pickles 74

Chicken Potatoes 74

Cracked-pepper Chicken Wings 75

Vegetables And Sides Recipes 75

Acorn Squash Slices 75

Flavourful Mexican Cauliflower 75

Kale And Spinach Chips 76

Lime Glazed Tofu 76

Brussels Sprouts 76

Fried Asparagus 76

Caprese Panini With Zucchini Chips 77

Healthy Air Fried Veggies 77

Falafel 78

Buffalo Bites 78

Green Beans With Baked Potatoes 78

Pepper Poppers 79

Fried Olives 79

Breaded Summer Squash 79

Air-fried Tofu Cutlets With Cacio E Pepe Brussels Sprouts 80

Sweet Potatoes & Brussels Sprouts 80

Chickpea Fritters 81

Potato And Parsnip Latkes With Baked Apples 81

Bbq Corn 82

Desserts Recipes 82

Sweet Potato Donut Holes 82

Fruity Blackberry Crisp 82

Pumpkin Hand Pies Blueberry Hand Pies 83

Citrus Mousse 83

Sweet Protein Powder Doughnut Holes 84

Zesty Cranberry Scones 84

Pineapple Wontons 84

Victoria Sponge Cake 85

Moist Chocolate Espresso Muffins 85

Monkey Bread 86

Gluten-free Spice Cookies 86

Chocolate Chip Cake 86

Churros 87

Speedy Chocolate Espresso Mini Cheesecake 87

Caramelized Fruit Skewers 87

Walnuts Fritters 88

Maple-pecan Tart With Sea Salt 88

Brownie Muffins 89

Lemon Raspberry Muffins 89

Berry Crumble And S'mores 89

Mocha Pudding Cake Vanilla Pudding Cake 90

Fluffy Layered Peanut Butter Cheesecake Brownies 90

Banana Spring Rolls With Hot Fudge Dip 91

Baked Apples 91

Soft Pecan Brownies 92

Air Fried Bananas 92

Pumpkin-spice Bread Pudding 92

Grilled Peaches 92

Pecan Brownies And Cinnamon-sugar Almonds 93

Easy Mini Chocolate Chip Pan Cookie 93

Bread Pudding 93

Snacks And Appetizers Recipes 94

Fried Halloumi Cheese 94

Bacon Wrapped Tater Tots 94

Chicken Stuffed Mushrooms 94

Onion Pakoras 95

Fried Pickles 95

Parmesan French Fries 95

Cinnamon Sugar Chickpeas 96

Tofu Veggie Meatballs 96

Tangy Fried Pickle Spears 96

Kale Potato Nuggets 97

Mozzarella Arancini 97

Crab Cakes 97

Fried Ravioli 97

Bacon-wrapped Shrimp And Jalapeño 98

Cheese Stuffed Mushrooms 98

Caramelized Onion Dip With White Cheese 98

Bruschetta With Basil Pesto 98

Crispy Filo Artichoke Triangles 99

"fried" Ravioli With Zesty Marinara 99

RECIPES INDEX 100

Breakfast Recipes

Spinach Egg Muffins

Servings: 4
Cooking Time: 13 Minutes.
Ingredients:
- 4 tablespoons milk
- 4 tablespoons frozen spinach, thawed
- 4 large eggs
- 8 teaspoons grated cheese
- Salt, to taste
- Black pepper, to taste
- Cooking Spray

Directions:
1. Grease four small-sized ramekin with cooking spray.
2. Add egg, cheese, spinach, and milk to a bowl and beat well.
3. Divide the mixture into the four small ramekins and top them with salt and black pepper.
4. Place the two ramekins in each of the two crisper plate.
5. Return the crisper plate to the Ninja Foodi Dual Zone Air Fryer.
6. Choose the Air Fry mode for Zone 1 and set the temperature to 390 degrees F and the time to 13 minutes.
7. Select the "MATCH" button to copy the settings for Zone 2.
8. Initiate cooking by pressing the START/STOP button.
9. Serve warm.

Nutrition:
- (Per serving) Calories 237 | Fat 19g | Sodium 518mg | Carbs 7g | Fiber 1.5g | Sugar 3.4g | Protein 12g

Cinnamon Apple French Toast

Servings: 8
Cooking Time: 10 Minutes
Ingredients:
- 1 egg, lightly beaten
- 4 bread slices
- 1 tbsp cinnamon
- 15ml milk
- 23ml maple syrup
- 45 ml applesauce

Directions:
1. In a bowl, whisk egg, milk, cinnamon, applesauce, and maple syrup.
2. Insert a crisper plate in the Ninja Foodi air fryer baskets.
3. Dip each slice in egg mixture and place in both baskets.
4. Select zone 1 then select "air fry" mode and set the temperature to 355 degrees F for 10 minutes. Press "match" to match zone 2 settings to zone 1. Press "start/stop" to begin.

Nutrition:
- (Per serving) Calories 64 | Fat 1.5g | Sodium 79mg | Carbs 10.8g | Fiber 1.3g | Sugar 4.8g | Protein 2.3g

Nutty Granola

Servings: 4
Cooking Time: 1 Hour
Ingredients:
- 120 ml pecans, coarsely chopped
- 120 ml walnuts or almonds, coarsely chopped
- 60 ml desiccated coconut
- 60 ml almond flour
- 60 ml ground flaxseed or chia seeds
- 2 tablespoons sunflower seeds
- 2 tablespoons melted butter
- 60 ml granulated sweetener
- ½ teaspoon ground cinnamon
- ½ teaspoon vanilla extract
- ¼ teaspoon ground nutmeg
- ¼ teaspoon salt
- 2 tablespoons water

Directions:
1. Preheat the air fryer to 120ºC. Cut a piece of parchment paper to fit inside the air fryer basket.
2. In a large bowl, toss the nuts, coconut, almond flour, ground flaxseed or chia seeds, sunflower seeds, butter, sweetener, cinnamon, vanilla, nutmeg, salt, and water until thoroughly combined.
3. Spread the granola on the parchment paper and flatten to an even thickness.
4. Air fry in the zone 1 air fryer basket for about an hour, or until golden throughout. Remove from the air fryer and allow to fully cool. Break the granola into bite-size pieces and store in a covered container for up to a week.

Cinnamon Toasts

Servings: 4
Cooking Time: 8 Minutes.
Ingredients:
- 4 pieces of bread
- 2 tablespoons butter
- 2 eggs, beaten
- 1 pinch salt
- 1 pinch cinnamon ground
- 1 pinch nutmeg ground
- 1 pinch ground clove
- 1 teaspoon icing sugar

Directions:
1. Add two eggs to a mixing bowl and stir cinnamon, nutmeg, ground cloves, and salt, then whisk well.
2. Spread butter on both sides of the bread slices and cut them into thick strips.
3. Dip the breadsticks in the egg mixture and place them in the two crisper plates.
4. Return the crisper plates to the Ninja Foodi Dual Zone Air Fryer.
5. Choose the Air Fry mode for Zone 1 and set the temperature to 390 degrees F and the time to 8 minutes.
6. Select the "MATCH" button to copy the settings for Zone 2.
7. Initiate cooking by pressing the START/STOP button.
8. Flip the French toast sticks when cooked halfway through.
9. Serve.

Nutrition:
- (Per serving) Calories 199 | Fat 11.1g |Sodium 297mg | Carbs 14.9g | Fiber 1g | Sugar 2.5g | Protein 9.9g

Sausage & Bacon Omelet

Servings: 4
Cooking Time: 10 Minutes
Ingredients:
- 8 eggs
- 2 bacon slices, chopped
- 4 sausages, chopped
- 2 yellow onions, chopped

Directions:
1. In a bowl, crack the eggs and beat well.
2. Add the remaining ingredients and gently stir to combine.
3. Divide the mixture into 2 small baking pans.
4. Press your chosen zone - "Zone 1" or "Zone 2" and then rotate the knob to select "Air Fry".
5. Set the temperature to 160 degrees C and then set the time for 5 minutes to preheat.
6. After preheating, arrange 1 pan into the basket of each zone.
7. Slide the basket into the Air Fryer and set the time for 10 minutes.
8. After cooking time is completed, remove the both pans from Air Fryer.
9. Cut each omelet in wedges and serve hot.

Wholemeal Banana-walnut Bread

Servings: 6
Cooking Time: 23 Minutes
Ingredients:
- Olive oil cooking spray
- 2 ripe medium bananas
- 1 large egg
- 60 ml non-fat plain Greek yoghurt
- 60 ml olive oil
- ½ teaspoon vanilla extract
- 2 tablespoons honey
- 235 ml wholemeal flour
- ¼ teaspoon salt
- ¼ teaspoon baking soda
- ½ teaspoon ground cinnamon
- 60 ml chopped walnuts

Directions:
1. Lightly coat the inside of two 5 ½-by-3-inch loaf pans with olive oil cooking spray.
2. In a large bowl, mash the bananas with a fork. Add the egg, yoghurt, olive oil, vanilla, and honey. Mix until well combined and mostly smooth. Sift the wholemeal flour, salt, baking soda, and cinnamon into the wet mixture, then stir until just combined. Do not overmix. Gently fold in the walnuts. Pour into the prepared loaf pans and spread to distribute evenly.
3. Place a loaf pan in the zone 1 drawer and another pan into zone 2 drawer. In zone 1, select Bake button and adjust temperature to 180ºC, set time to 20 to 23 minutes. In zone 2, select Match Cook and press Start.
4. Remove until golden brown on top and a toothpick inserted into the center comes out clean. Allow to cool for 5 minutes before serving.

Egg In Bread Hole

Servings: 1
Cooking Time: 8 Minutes
Ingredients:
- 1 tablespoon butter, softened
- 2 eggs
- 2 slices of bread
- Salt and black pepper, to taste

Directions:
1. Line either basket of "Zone 1" and "Zone 2" with a greased piece of foil.
2. Press your chosen zone - "Zone 1" or "Zone 2" and then rotate the knob to select "Air Fryer".
3. Set the temperature to 160 degrees C, and then set the time for 3 minutes to preheat.
4. After preheating, place the butter on both sides of the bread. Cut a hole in the centre of the bread and crack the egg.
5. Slide the basket into the Air Fryer and set the time for 6 minutes.
6. After cooking time is completed, transfer the bread to a serving plate and serve.

Mozzarella Bacon Calzones

Servings: 4
Cooking Time: 12 Minutes
Ingredients:
- 2 large eggs
- 235 ml blanched finely ground almond flour
- 475 ml shredded Mozzarella cheese
- 60 g cream cheese, softened and broken into small pieces
- 4 slices cooked bacon, crumbled

Directions:
1. Beat eggs in a small bowl. Pour into a medium nonstick skillet over medium heat and scramble. Set aside.
2. In a large microwave-safe bowl, mix flour and Mozzarella. Add cream cheese to the bowl.
3. Place bowl in microwave and cook 45 seconds on high to melt cheese, then stir with a fork until a soft dough ball forms.
4. Cut a piece of parchment to fit air fryer drawer. Separate dough into two sections and press each out into an 8-inch round.
5. On half of each dough round, place half of the scrambled eggs and crumbled bacon. Fold the other side of the dough over and press to seal the edges.
6. Place calzones on ungreased parchment and into the zone 1 air fryer drawer. Adjust the temperature to 176ºC and set the timer for 12 minutes, turning calzones halfway through cooking. Crust will be golden and firm when done.
7. Let calzones cool on a cooking rack 5 minutes before serving.

Egg White Muffins

Servings: 8
Cooking Time: 10 Minutes
Ingredients:
- 4 slices center-cut bacon, cut into strips
- 4 ounces baby bella mushrooms, roughly chopped
- 2 ounces sun-dried tomatoes
- 2 tablespoon sliced black olives
- 2 tablespoons grated or shredded parmesan
- 2 tablespoons shredded mozzarella
- ¼ teaspoon black pepper
- ¾ cup liquid egg whites
- 2 tablespoons liquid egg whites

Directions:
1. Heat a saucepan with a little oil, add the bacon and mushrooms and cook until fully cooked and crispy, about 6–8 minutes.
2. While the bacon and mushrooms cook, mix the ¾ cup liquid egg whites, sun-dried tomato, olives, parmesan, mozzarella, and black pepper together in a large bowl.
3. Add the cooked bacon and mushrooms to the tomato and olive mixture, stirring everything together.
4. Spoon the mixture into muffin molds, followed by 2 tablespoons of egg whites over the top.
5. Place half the muffins mold in zone 1 and half in zone 2, then insert the drawers into the unit.
6. Select zone 1, select AIR FRY, set temperature to 390 degrees F/ 200 degrees C, and set time to 22 minutes.
7. Select MATCH to match zone 2 settings to zone 1. Press the START/STOP button to begin cooking.
8. When cooking is complete, remove the molds and enjoy!

Nutrition:
- (Per serving) Calories 104 | Fat 5.6g | Sodium 269mg | Carbs 3.5g | Fiber 0.8g | Sugar 0.3g | Protein 10.3g

Sausage And Cheese Balls

Servings: 16 Balls
Cooking Time: 12 Minutes
Ingredients:
- 450 g pork sausage meat, removed from casings
- 120 ml shredded Cheddar cheese
- 30 g full-fat cream cheese, softened
- 1 large egg

Directions:
1. Mix all ingredients in a large bowl. Form into sixteen balls. Place the balls into the two air fryer drawers.
2. Adjust the temperature to 204°C and air fry for 12 minutes.
3. Shake the drawers two or three times during cooking. Sausage balls will be browned on the outside and have an internal temperature of at least 64°C when completely cooked.
4. Serve warm.

Pepper Egg Cups

Servings: 4
Cooking Time: 18 Minutes.
Ingredients:
- 2 halved bell pepper, seeds removed
- 4 eggs
- 1 teaspoon olive oil
- 1 pinch salt and black pepper
- 1 pinch sriracha flakes

Directions:
1. Slice the bell peppers in half, lengthwise, and remove their seeds and the inner portion to get a cup-like shape.
2. Rub olive oil on the edges of the bell peppers.
3. Place them in the two crisper plates with their cut side up and crack 1 egg in each half of bell pepper.
4. Drizzle salt, black pepper, and sriracha flakes on top of the eggs.
5. Return the crisper plates to the Ninja Foodi Dual Zone Air Fryer.
6. Choose the Air Fry mode for Zone 1 and set the temperature to 390 degrees F and the time to 18 minutes.
7. Select the "MATCH" button to copy the settings for Zone 2.
8. Initiate cooking by pressing the START/STOP button.
9. Serve warm and fresh.

Nutrition:
- (Per serving) Calories 183 | Fat 15g | Sodium 402mg | Carbs 2.5g | Fiber 0.4g | Sugar 1.1g | Protein 10g

Sausage And Egg Breakfast Burrito

Servings: 6
Cooking Time: 30 Minutes
Ingredients:
- 6 eggs
- Salt and pepper, to taste
- Cooking oil
- 120 ml chopped red pepper
- 120 ml chopped green pepper
- 230 g chicken sausage meat (removed from casings)
- 120 ml salsa
- 6 medium (8-inch) flour tortillas
- 120 ml shredded Cheddar cheese

Directions:
1. In a medium bowl, whisk the eggs. Add salt and pepper to taste.
2. Place a skillet on medium-high heat. Spray with cooking oil. Add the eggs. Scramble for 2 to 3 minutes, until the eggs are fluffy. Remove the eggs from the skillet and set aside.
3. If needed, spray the skillet with more oil. Add the chopped red and green bell peppers. Cook for 2 to 3 minutes, until the peppers are soft.
4. Add the sausage meat to the skillet. Break the sausage into smaller pieces using a spatula or spoon. Cook for 3 to 4 minutes, until the sausage is brown.
5. Add the salsa and scrambled eggs. Stir to combine. Remove the skillet from heat.
6. Spoon the mixture evenly onto the tortillas.
7. To form the burritos, fold the sides of each tortilla in toward the middle and then roll up from the bottom. You can secure each burrito with a toothpick. Or you can moisten the outside edge of the tortilla with a small amount of water. I prefer to use a cooking brush, but you can also dab with your fingers.
8. Spray the burritos with cooking oil and place them in the two air fryer drawers. Do not stack. Air fry at 204°C for 8 minutes.
9. Open the air fryer and flip the burritos. Cook for an additional 2 minutes or until crisp.
10. Sprinkle the Cheddar cheese over the burritos. Cool before serving.

Breakfast Sausage Omelet

Servings: 2
Cooking Time: 8
Ingredients:
- ¼ pound breakfast sausage, cooked and crumbled
- 4 eggs, beaten
- ½ cup pepper Jack cheese blend
- 2 tablespoons green bell pepper, sliced
- 1 green onion, chopped
- 1 pinch cayenne pepper
- Cooking spray

Directions:
1. Take a bowl and whisk eggs in it along with crumbled sausage, pepper Jack cheese, green onions, red bell pepper, and cayenne pepper.
2. Mix it all well.
3. Take two cake pans that fit inside the air fryer and grease it with oil spray.
4. Divide the omelet mixture between cake pans.
5. Put the cake pans inside both of the Ninja Foodie 2-Basket Air Fryer baskets.
6. Turn on the BAKE function of the zone 1 basket and let it cook for 15-20 minutes at 310 degrees F.
7. Select MATCH button for zone 2 basket.
8. Once the cooking cycle completes, take out, and serve hot, as a delicious breakfast.

Nutrition:
- (Per serving) Calories 691| Fat52.4g | Sodium1122 mg | Carbs 13.3g | Fiber 1.8g| Sugar 7g | Protein 42g

Honey Banana Oatmeal

Servings: 4
Cooking Time: 8 Minutes
Ingredients:
- 2 eggs
- 2 tbsp honey
- 1 tsp vanilla
- 45g quick oats
- 73ml milk
- 30g Greek yoghurt
- 219g banana, mashed

Directions:
1. In a bowl, mix eggs, milk, yoghurt, honey, vanilla, oats, and mashed banana until well combined.
2. Pour batter into the four greased ramekins.
3. Insert a crisper plate in the Ninja Foodi air fryer baskets.
4. Place ramekins in both baskets.
5. Select zone 1 then select "air fry" mode and set the temperature to 390 degrees F for 8 minutes. Press "match" to match zone 2 settings to zone 1. Press "start/stop" to begin.

Nutrition:
- (Per serving) Calories 228 | Fat 4.6g |Sodium 42mg | Carbs 40.4g | Fiber 4.2g | Sugar 16.1g | Protein 7.7g

Egg And Avocado In The Ninja Foodi

Servings: 2
Cooking Time: 12
Ingredients:
- 2 Avocados, pitted and cut in half
- Garlic salt, to taste
- Cooking for greasing
- 4 eggs
- ¼ teaspoon of Paprika powder, for sprinkling
- 1/3 cup parmesan cheese, crumbled
- 6 bacon strips, raw

Directions:
1. First cut the avocado in half and pit it.
2. Now scoop out the flesh from the avocado and keep intact some of it
3. Crack one egg in each hole of avocado and sprinkle paprika and garlic salt
4. Top it with cheese at the end.
5. Now put it into tin foils and then put it in the air fryer zone basket 1
6. Put bacon strips in zone 2 basket.
7. Now for zone 1, set it to AIR FRY mode at 350 degrees F for 10 minutes
8. And for zone 2, set it 400 degrees for 12 minutes AIR FRY mode.
9. Press the Smart finish button and press start, it will finish both at the same time.
10. Once done, serve and enjoy.

Nutrition:
- (Per serving) Calories609 | Fat53.2g | Sodium 335mg | Carbs 18.1g | Fiber13.5g | Sugar 1.7g | Protein 21.3g

Sausage & Butternut Squash

Servings: 2
Cooking Time: 20 Minutes
Ingredients:
- 450g butternut squash, diced
- 70g kielbasa, diced
- ¼ onion, diced
- ¼ tsp garlic powder
- ½ tbsp olive oil
- Pepper
- Salt

Directions:
1. In a bowl, toss butternut squash with garlic powder, oil, onion, kielbasa, pepper, and salt.
2. Insert a crisper plate in the Ninja Foodi air fryer baskets.
3. Add sausage and butternut squash mixture in both baskets.
4. Select zone 1, then select "air fry" mode and set the temperature to 375 degrees F for 20 minutes. Press "match" to match zone 2 settings to zone 1. Press "start/stop" to begin. Stir halfway through.

Nutrition:
- (Per serving) Calories 68 | Fat 3.6g | Sodium 81mg | Carbs 9.7g | Fiber 1.7g | Sugar 2.2g | Protein 0.9g

Bacon Cheese Egg With Avocado And Potato Nuggets

Servings: 8
Cooking Time: 20 Minutes
Ingredients:
- Bacon Cheese Egg with Avocado:
- 6 large eggs
- 60 ml double cream
- 350 ml chopped cauliflower
- 235 ml shredded medium Cheddar cheese
- 1 medium avocado, peeled and pitted
- 8 tablespoons full-fat sour cream
- 2 spring onions, sliced on the bias
- 12 slices bacon, cooked and crumbled
- Potato Nuggets:
- 1 teaspoon extra virgin olive oil
- 1 clove garlic, minced
- 1 L kale, rinsed and chopped
- 475 ml potatoes, boiled and mashed
- 30 ml milk
- Salt and ground black pepper, to taste
- Cooking spray

Directions:
1. Make the Bacon Cheese Egg with Avocado :
2. In a medium bowl, whisk eggs and cream together. Pour into a round baking dish.
3. Add cauliflower and mix, then top with Cheddar. Place dish into the zone 1 air fryer drawer.
4. Adjust the temperature to 160°C and set the timer for 20 minutes.
5. When completely cooked, eggs will be firm and cheese will be browned. Slice into four pieces.
6. Slice avocado and divide evenly among pieces. Top each piece with 2 tablespoons sour cream, sliced spring onions, and crumbled bacon.
7. Make the Potato Nuggets :
8. Preheat the zone 2 air fryer drawer to 200°C.
9. In a skillet over medium heat, sauté the garlic in the olive oil, until it turns golden brown. Sauté with the kale for an additional 3 minutes and remove from the heat.
10. Mix the mashed potatoes, kale and garlic in a bowl. Pour in the milk and sprinkle with salt and pepper.
11. Shape the mixture into nuggets and spritz with cooking spray.
12. Put in the zone 2 air fryer drawer and air fry for 15 minutes, flip the nuggets halfway through cooking to make sure the nuggets fry evenly.
13. Serve immediately.

Eggs In Avocado Cups

Servings: 4
Cooking Time: 12 Minutes
Ingredients:
- 2 avocados, halved and pitted
- 4 eggs
- Salt and ground black pepper, as required

Directions:
1. Line either basket of "Zone 1" and "Zone 2" of Ninja Foodi 2-Basket Air Fryer with a greased square piece of foil.
2. Press your chosen zone - "Zone 1" and "Zone 2" and then rotate the knob to select "Bake".
3. Set the temperature to 200 degrees C and then set the time for 5 minutes to preheat.
4. Meanwhile, carefully scoop out about 2 teaspoons of flesh from each avocado half.
5. Crack 1 egg in each avocado half and sprinkle with salt and black pepper.
6. After preheating, arrange 2 avocado halves into the basket.
7. Slide the basket into the Air Fryer and set the time for 12 minutes.
8. After cooking time is completed, transfer the avocado halves and onto serving plates and serve hot.

Gyro Breakfast Patties With Tzatziki

Servings: 16
Cooking Time: 20 Minutes
Ingredients:
- patties
- Patties:
- 900 g lamb or beef mince
- 120 ml diced red onions
- 60 ml sliced black olives
- 2 tablespoons tomato sauce
- 1 teaspoon dried oregano leaves
- 2 cloves garlic, minced
- 1 teaspoon fine sea salt
- Tzatziki:
- 235 ml full-fat sour cream
- 1 small cucumber, chopped
- ½ teaspoon fine sea salt
- ½ teaspoon garlic powder, or 1 clove garlic, minced
- ¼ teaspoon dried dill, or 1 teaspoon finely chopped fresh dill
- For Garnish/Serving:
- 120 ml crumbled feta cheese (about 60 g)
- Diced red onions
- Sliced black olives
- Sliced cucumbers

Directions:
1. Preheat the air fryer to 176°C. 2. Place the lamb, onions, olives, tomato sauce, oregano, garlic, and salt in a large bowl. Mix well to combine the ingredients. 3. Using your hands, form the mixture into sixteen 3-inch patties. Place the patties in the two air fryer drawers and air fry for 20 minutes, flipping halfway through. Remove the patties and place them on a serving platter. 4. While the patties cook, make the tzatziki: Place all the ingredients in a small bowl and stir well. Cover and store in the fridge until ready to serve. Garnish with ground black pepper before serving. 5. Serve the patties with a dollop of tzatziki, a sprinkle of crumbled feta cheese, diced red onions, sliced black olives, and sliced cucumbers. 6. Store leftovers in an airtight container in the refrigerator for up to 5 days or in the freezer for up to a month. Reheat the patties in a preheated 200°C air fryer for a few minutes, until warmed through.

Easy Pancake Doughnuts

Servings: 8
Cooking Time: 9 Minutes
Ingredients:
- 2 eggs
- 50g sugar
- 125ml vegetable oil
- 240g pancake mix
- 1 ½ tbsp cinnamon

Directions:
1. In a bowl, mix pancake mix, eggs, cinnamon, sugar, and oil until well combined.
2. Pour the doughnut mixture into the silicone doughnut moulds.
3. Insert a crisper plate in Ninja Foodi air fryer baskets.
4. Place doughnut moulds in both baskets.
5. Select zone 1 then select "air fry" mode and set the temperature to 355 degrees F for 9 minutes. Press "match" to match zone 2 settings to zone 1. Press "start/stop" to begin.

Nutrition:
- (Per serving) Calories 163 | Fat 14.7g | Sodium 16mg | Carbs 7.4g | Fiber 0.7g | Sugar 6.4g | Protein 1.4g

Air Fryer Sausage Patties

Servings: 12
Cooking Time: 10 Minutes
Ingredients:
- 1-pound pork sausage or ready-made patties
- Fennel seeds or preferred seasonings

Directions:
1. Prepare the sausage by slicing it into patties, then flavor it with fennel seed or your favorite seasonings.
2. Install a crisper plate in both drawers. Place half the patties in zone 1 and half in zone 2, then insert the drawers into the unit.
3. Select zone 1, select AIR FRY, set temperature to 390 degrees F/ 200 degrees C, and set time to 10 minutes.
4. Select MATCH to match zone 2 settings to zone 1.
5. Press the START/STOP button to begin cooking.
6. When cooking is complete, remove the patties from the unit and serve with sauce or make a burger.

Nutrition:
- (Per serving) Calories 130 | Fat 10.5g | Sodium 284mg | Carbs 0.3g | Fiber 0.2g | Sugar 0g | Protein 7.4g

Yellow Potatoes With Eggs

Servings: 2
Cooking Time: 35
Ingredients:
- 1 pound of Dutch yellow potatoes, quartered
- 1 red bell pepper, chopped
- Salt and black pepper, to taste
- 1 green bell pepper, chopped
- 2 teaspoons of olive oil
- 2 teaspoons of garlic powder
- 1 teaspoon of onion powder
- 1 egg
- ¼ teaspoon of butter

Directions:
1. Toss together diced potatoes, green pepper, red pepper, salt, black pepper, and olive oil along with garlic powder and onion powder.
2. Put in the zone 1 basket of the air fryer.
3. Take ramekin and grease it with oil spray.
4. Whisk egg in a bowl and add salt and pepper along with ½ teaspoon of butter.
5. Pour egg into a ramekin and place it in a zone 2 basket.
6. Now start cooking and set a timer for zone 1 basket to 30-35 minutes at 400 degrees at AIR FRY mode.
7. Now for zone 2, set it on AIR FRY mode at 350 degrees F for 8-10 minutes.
8. Press the Smart finish button and press start, it will finish both at the same time.
9. Once done, serve and enjoy.

Nutrition:
- (Per serving) Calories 252 | Fat 7.5g | Sodium 37mg | Carbs 40g | Fiber 3.9g | Sugar 7g | Protein 6.7g

Wholemeal Blueberry Muffins

Servings: 6
Cooking Time: 15 Minutes
Ingredients:
- Olive oil cooking spray
- 120 ml unsweetened applesauce
- 60 ml honey
- 120 ml non-fat plain Greek yoghurt
- 1 teaspoon vanilla extract
- 1 large egg
- 350 ml plus 1 tablespoon wholemeal, divided
- ½ teaspoon baking soda
- ½ teaspoon baking powder
- ½ teaspoon salt
- 120 ml blueberries, fresh or frozen

Directions:
1. Lightly coat the inside of six silicone muffin cups or a six-cup muffin tin with olive oil cooking spray.
2. In a large bowl, combine the applesauce, honey, yoghurt, vanilla, and egg and mix until smooth. Sift in 350 ml of the flour, the baking soda, baking powder, and salt into the wet mixture, then stir until just combined. In a small bowl, toss the blueberries with the remaining 1 tablespoon flour, then fold the mixture into the muffin batter.
3. Divide the mixture evenly among the prepared muffin cups and place into the zone 1 drawer of the air fryer. Bake at 182°C for 12 to 15 minutes, or until golden brown on top and a toothpick inserted into the middle of one of the muffins comes out clean. Allow to cool for 5 minutes before serving.

Cinnamon Rolls

Servings: 12 Rolls
Cooking Time: 20 Minutes
Ingredients:
- 600 ml shredded Mozzarella cheese
- 60 g cream cheese, softened
- 235 ml blanched finely ground almond flour
- ½ teaspoon vanilla extract
- 120 ml icing sugar-style sweetener
- 1 tablespoon ground cinnamon

Directions:
1. In a large microwave-safe bowl, combine Mozzarella cheese, cream cheese, and flour. Microwave the mixture on high 90 seconds until cheese is melted.
2. Add vanilla extract and sweetener, and mix 2 minutes until a dough forms.
3. Once the dough is cool enough to work with your hands, about 2 minutes, spread it out into a 12 × 4-inch rectangle on ungreased parchment paper. Evenly sprinkle dough with cinnamon.
4. Starting at the long side of the dough, roll lengthwise to form a log. Slice the log into twelve even pieces.
5. Divide rolls between two ungreased round nonstick baking dishes. Place the dishes into the two air fryer drawers. Adjust the temperature to 192°C and bake for 10 minutes.
6. Cinnamon rolls will be done when golden around the edges and mostly firm. Allow rolls to cool in dishes 10 minutes before serving.

Banana Bread

Servings: 8
Cooking Time: 35 Minutes
Ingredients:
- 95g flour
- 1 teaspoon ground cinnamon
- ¼ teaspoon ground nutmeg
- ½ teaspoon salt
- ¼ teaspoon baking soda
- 2 medium-sized ripe bananas mashed
- 2 large eggs lightly beaten
- 100g granulated sugar
- 2 tablespoons whole milk
- 1 tablespoon plain nonfat yoghurt
- 2 tablespoons vegetable oil
- 1 teaspoon vanilla
- 2 tablespoons walnuts roughly chopped

Directions:
1. Combine flour, cinnamon, nutmeg, baking soda, and salt in a large mixing basin.
2. Mash the banana in a separate dish before adding the eggs, sugar, milk, yoghurt, oil, and vanilla extract.
3. Combine the wet and dry ingredients in a mixing bowl and stir until just incorporated.
4. Pour the batter into the loaf pan and top with chopped walnuts.
5. Press either "Zone 1" and "Zone 2" and then rotate the knob select "Air Fryer".
6. Set the temperature to 155 degrees C, and then set the time for 3 minutes to preheat.
7. After preheating, arrange 1 loaf pan into the basket.
8. Slide basket into Air Fryer and set the time for 35 minutes.
9. After cooking time is completed, remove pan from Air Fryer.
10. Place the loaf pan onto a wire rack to cool for about 10 minutes.
11. Carefully invert the bread onto a wire rack to cool completely before slicing
12. Cut the bread into desired-sized slices and serve.

Quiche Breakfast Peppers

Servings: 4
Cooking Time: 15 Minutes
Ingredients:
- 4 eggs
- ½ tsp garlic powder
- 112g mozzarella cheese, shredded
- 125g ricotta cheese
- 2 bell peppers, cut in half & remove seeds
- 7½g baby spinach, chopped
- 22g parmesan cheese, grated
- ¼ tsp dried parsley

Directions:
1. In a bowl, whisk eggs, ricotta cheese, garlic powder, parsley, cheese, and spinach.
2. Pour the egg mixture into each bell pepper half and top with mozzarella cheese.
3. Insert a crisper plate in the Ninja Foodi air fryer baskets.
4. Place bell peppers in both the baskets.
5. Select zone 1 then select "air fry" mode and set the temperature to 355 degrees F for 15 minutes. Press "match" to match zone 2 settings to zone 1. Press "start/stop" to begin.

Nutrition:
- (Per serving) Calories 136 | Fat 7.6g | Sodium 125mg | Carbs 6.9g | Fiber 0.9g | Sugar 3.5g | Protein 10.8g

Egg And Bacon Muffins

Servings: 1
Cooking Time: 15 Minutes
Ingredients:
- 2 eggs
- Salt and ground black pepper, to taste
- 1 tablespoon green pesto
- 85 g shredded Cheddar cheese
- 140 g cooked bacon
- 1 spring onion, chopped

Directions:
1. Line a cupcake tin with parchment paper. Beat the eggs with pepper, salt, and pesto in a bowl. Mix in the cheese.
2. Pour the eggs into the cupcake tin and top with the bacon and spring onion.
3. Place the cupcake tin into the zone 1 drawer and bake at 180°C for 15 minutes, or until the egg is set. Serve immediately.

Baked Mushroom And Mozzarella Frittata With Breakfast Potatoes

Servings: 4
Cooking Time: 35 Minutes
Ingredients:
- FOR THE FRITTATA
- 8 large eggs
- ⅓ cup whole milk
- 1 teaspoon kosher salt
- ½ teaspoon freshly ground black pepper
- 1 cup sliced cremini mushrooms (about 2 ounces)
- 1 teaspoon olive oil
- 2 ounces part-skim mozzarella cheese, cut into ½-inch cubes
- FOR THE POTATOES
- 2 russet potatoes, cut into ½-inch cubes
- 1 tablespoon olive oil
- ½ teaspoon garlic powder
- ¼ teaspoon kosher salt
- ¼ teaspoon freshly ground black pepper

Directions:
1. To prep the frittata: In a large bowl, whisk together the eggs, milk, salt, and pepper. Stir in the mushrooms.
2. To prep the potatoes: In a large bowl, combine the potatoes, olive oil, garlic powder, salt, and black pepper.
3. To cook the frittata and potatoes: Brush the bottom of the Zone 1 basket with 1 teaspoon of olive oil. Add the egg mixture to the basket, top with the mozzarella cubes, and insert the basket in the unit. Install a crisper plate in the Zone 2 basket. Place the potatoes in the basket and insert the basket in the unit.
4. Select Zone 1, select BAKE, set the temperature to 350°F, and set the time to 30 minutes.
5. Select Zone 2, select AIR FRY, set the temperature to 400°F, and set the time to 35 minutes. Select SMART FINISH.
6. Press START/PAUSE to begin cooking.
7. When the Zone 2 timer reads 15 minutes, press START/PAUSE. Remove the basket and shake the potatoes for 10 seconds. Reinsert the basket and press START/PAUSE to resume cooking.
8. When cooking is complete, the frittata will pull away from the edges of the basket and the potatoes will be golden brown. Transfer the frittata to a cutting board and cut into 4 portions. Serve with the potatoes.

Nutrition:
- (Per serving) Calories: 307; Total fat: 17g; Saturated fat: 5.5g; Carbohydrates: 18g; Fiber: 1g; Protein: 19g; Sodium: 600mg

Vanilla Strawberry Doughnuts

Servings: 8
Cooking Time: 15 Minutes
Ingredients:
- 1 egg
- ½ cup strawberries, diced
- 80ml cup milk
- 1 tsp cinnamon
- 1 tsp baking soda
- 136g all-purpose flour
- 2 tsp vanilla
- 2 tbsp butter, melted
- 73g sugar
- ½ tsp salt

Directions:
1. In a bowl, mix flour, cinnamon, baking soda, sugar, and salt.
2. In a separate bowl, whisk egg, milk, butter, and vanilla.
3. Pour egg mixture into the flour mixture and mix until well combined.
4. Add strawberries and mix well.
5. Pour batter into the silicone doughnut moulds.
6. Insert a crisper plate in the Ninja Foodi air fryer baskets.
7. Place doughnut moulds in both baskets.
8. Select zone 1, then select "air fry" mode and set the temperature to 320 degrees F for 15 minutes. Press "match" to match zone 2 settings to zone 1. Press "start/stop" to begin.

Nutrition:
- (Per serving) Calories 133 | Fat 3.8g |Sodium 339mg | Carbs 21.9g | Fiber 0.8g | Sugar 9.5g | Protein 2.7g

Donuts

Servings: 6
Cooking Time: 15 Minutes
Ingredients:
- 1 cup granulated sugar
- 2 tablespoons ground cinnamon
- 1 can refrigerated flaky buttermilk biscuits
- ¼ cup unsalted butter, melted

Directions:
1. Combine the sugar and cinnamon in a small shallow bowl and set aside.
2. Remove the biscuits from the can and put them on a chopping board, separated. Cut holes in the center of each biscuit with a 1-inch round biscuit cutter (or a similarly sized bottle cap).
3. Place a crisper plate in each drawer. In each drawer, place 4 biscuits in a single layer. Insert the drawers into the unit.
4. Select zone 1, then AIR FRY, then set the temperature to 360 degrees F/ 180 degrees C with a 10-minute timer. To match zone 2 settings to zone 1, choose MATCH. To begin cooking, select START/STOP.
5. Remove the donuts from the drawers after the timer has finished.

Nutrition:
- (Per serving) Calories 223 | Fat 8g | Sodium 150mg | Carbs 40g | Fiber 1.4g | Sugar 34.2g | Protein 0.8g

Cinnamon-raisin Bagels

Everything Bagels

Servings: 4
Cooking Time: 14 Minutes
Ingredients:
- FOR THE BAGEL DOUGH
- 1 cup all-purpose flour, plus more for dusting
- 2 teaspoons baking powder
- 1 teaspoon kosher salt
- 1 cup reduced-fat plain Greek yogurt
- FOR THE CINNAMON-RAISIN BAGELS
- ¼ cup raisins
- ½ teaspoon ground cinnamon
- FOR THE EVERYTHING BAGELS
- ¼ teaspoon poppy seeds
- ¼ teaspoon sesame seeds
- ¼ teaspoon dried minced garlic
- ¼ teaspoon dried minced onion
- FOR THE EGG WASH
- 1 large egg
- 1 tablespoon water

Directions:
1. To prep the bagels: In a large bowl, combine the flour, baking powder, and salt. Stir in the yogurt to form a soft dough. Turn the dough out onto a lightly floured surface and knead five to six times, until it is smooth and elastic. Divide the dough in half.
2. Knead the raisins and cinnamon into one dough half. Leave the other dough half plain.
3. Divide both portions of dough in half to form a total of 4 balls of dough (2 cinnamon-raisin and 2 plain). Roll each ball of dough into a rope about 8 inches long. Shape each rope into a ring and pinch the ends to seal.
4. To prep the everything bagels: In a small bowl, mix together the poppy seeds, sesame seeds, garlic, and onion.
5. To prep the egg wash: In a second small bowl, beat together the egg and water. Brush the egg wash on top of each bagel.
6. Generously sprinkle the everything seasoning over the top of the 2 plain bagels.
7. To cook the bagels: Install a crisper plate in each of the two baskets. Place the cinnamon-raisin bagels in the Zone 1 basket and insert the basket in the unit. For best results, the bagels should not overlap in the basket. Place the everything bagels in the Zone 2 basket and insert the basket in the unit.
8. Select Zone 1, select AIR FRY, set the temperature to 325°F, and set the time to 14 minutes. Select MATCH COOK to match Zone 2 settings to Zone 1.
9. Press START/PAUSE to begin cooking.
10. When cooking is complete, use silicone-tipped tongs to transfer the bagels to a cutting board. Let cool for 2 to 3 minutes before cutting and serving.

Nutrition:
- (Per serving) Calories: 238; Total fat: 3g; Saturated fat: 1g; Carbohydrates: 43g; Fiber: 1.5g; Protein: 11g; Sodium: 321mg

Canadian Bacon Muffin Sandwiches And All-in-one Toast

Servings: 5
Cooking Time: 10 Minutes
Ingredients:
- Canadian Bacon Muffin Sandwiches:
- 4 English muffins, split
- 8 slices back bacon
- 4 slices cheese
- Cooking spray
- All-in-One Toast:
- 1 strip bacon, diced
- 1 slice 1-inch thick bread
- 1 egg
- Salt and freshly ground black pepper, to taste
- 60 ml grated Monterey Jack or Chedday cheese

Directions:
1. Make the Canadian Bacon Muffin Sandwiches :
2. 1. Preheat the air fryer to 190°C. Make the sandwiches: Top each of 4 muffin halves with 2 slices of bacon, 1 slice of cheese, and finish with the remaining muffin half. 3. Put the sandwiches in the zone 1 air fryer basket and spritz the tops with cooking spray. 4. Bake for 4 minutes. Flip the sandwiches and bake for another 4 minutes. 5. Divide the sandwiches among four plates and serve warm.
3. Make the All-in-One Toast :
4. Preheat the air fryer to 205°C.
5. Air fry the bacon in zone 2 basket for 3 minutes, shaking the basket once or twice while it cooks. Remove the bacon to a paper towel lined plate and set aside.
6. Use a sharp paring knife to score a large circle in the middle of the slice of bread, cutting halfway through, but not all the way through to the cutting board. Press down on the circle in the center of the bread slice to create an indentation.
7. Transfer the slice of bread, hole side up, to the zone 2 air fryer basket. Crack the egg into the center of the bread, and season with salt and pepper.
8. Adjust the air fryer temperature to 190°C and air fry for 5 minutes. Sprinkle the grated cheese around the edges of the bread, leaving the center of the yolk uncovered, and top with the cooked bacon. Press the cheese and bacon into the bread lightly to help anchor it to the bread and prevent it from blowing around in the air fryer.
9. Air fry for one or two more minutes, just to melt the cheese and finish cooking the egg. Serve immediately.

Breakfast Potatoes

Servings: 6
Cooking Time: 20 Minutes
Ingredients:
- 3 russet potatoes, cut into bite-sized pieces with skin on
- 1 teaspoon garlic powder
- 1 teaspoon onion powder
- 2 teaspoons fine ground sea salt
- 1 teaspoon black pepper
- 1 tablespoon olive oil
- ½ red pepper, diced

Directions:
1. The potatoes should be washed and scrubbed before being sliced into bite-sized pieces with the skin on.
2. Using paper towels, dry them and place them in a large mixing bowl.
3. Toss in the spices and drizzle with olive oil. Stir in the pepper until everything is completely combined.
4. Line a basket with parchment paper.
5. Press either "Zone 1" or "Zone 2" and then rotate the knob to select "Air Fryer".
6. Set the temperature to 195 degrees C, and then set the time for 3 minutes to preheat.
7. After preheating, spread the potatoes in a single layer on the sheet.
8. Slide basket into Air Fryer and set the time for 15 minutes.
9. After cooking time is completed, remove basket from Air Fryer.
10. Place them on serving plates and serve.

Asparagus And Bell Pepper Strata And Greek Bagels

Servings: 6
Cooking Time: 14 To 20 Minutes
Ingredients:
- Asparagus and Bell Pepper Strata:
- 8 large asparagus spears, trimmed and cut into 2-inch pieces
- 80 ml shredded carrot
- 120 ml chopped red pepper
- 2 slices wholemeal bread, cut into ½-inch cubes
- 3 egg whites
- 1 egg
- 3 tablespoons 1% milk
- ½ teaspoon dried thyme
- Greek Bagels:
- 120 ml self-raising flour, plus more for dusting
- 120 ml plain Greek yoghurt
- 1 egg
- 1 tablespoon water
- 4 teaspoons sesame seeds or za'atar
- Cooking oil spray
- 1 tablespoon butter, melted

Directions:
1. Make the Asparagus and Bell Pepper Strata :
2. In a baking pan, combine the asparagus, carrot, red bell pepper, and 1 tablespoon of water. Bake in the air fryer at 166°C for 3 to 5 minutes, or until crisp-tender. Drain well.
3. Add the bread cubes to the vegetables and gently toss.
4. In a medium bowl, whisk the egg whites, egg, milk, and thyme until frothy.
5. Pour the egg mixture into the pan. Bake in the zone 1 drawer for 11 to 15 minutes, or until the strata is slightly puffy and set and the top starts to brown. Serve.
6. Make the Greek Bagels :
7. In a large bowl, using a wooden spoon, stir together the flour and yoghurt until a tacky dough forms. Transfer the dough to a lightly floured work surface and roll the dough into a ball.
8. Cut the dough into 2 pieces and roll each piece into a log. Form each log into a bagel shape, pinching the ends together.
9. In a small bowl, whisk the egg and water. Brush the egg wash on the bagels.
10. Sprinkle 2 teaspoons of the toppings on each bagel and gently press it into the dough.
11. Insert the crisper plate into the zone 2 drawer and the drawer into the unit. Preheat the drawer by selecting BAKE, setting the temperature to 166°C, and setting the time to 3 minutes. Select START/STOP to begin.
12. Once the drawer is preheated, spray the crisper plate with cooking spray. Drizzle the bagels with the butter and place them into the drawer.
13. Select BAKE, set the temperature to 166°C, and set the time to 10 minutes. Select START/STOP to begin.
14. When the cooking is complete, the bagels should be lightly golden on the outside. Serve warm.

Morning Patties

Servings: 4
Cooking Time: 13 Minutes.
Ingredients:
- 1 lb. minced pork
- 1 lb. minced turkey
- 2 teaspoons dry rubbed sage
- 2 teaspoons fennel seeds
- 2 teaspoons garlic powder
- 1 teaspoon paprika
- 1 teaspoon of sea salt
- 1 teaspoon dried thyme

Directions:
1. In a mixing bowl, add turkey and pork, then mix them together.
2. Mix sage, fennel, paprika, salt, thyme, and garlic powder in a small bowl.
3. Drizzle this mixture over the meat mixture and mix well.
4. Take 2 tablespoons of this mixture at a time and roll it into thick patties.
5. Place half of the patties in Zone 1, and the other half in Zone 2, then spray them all with cooking oil.
6. Return the crisper plate to the Ninja Foodi Dual Zone Air Fryer.
7. Choose the Air Fry mode for Zone 1 and set the temperature to 390 degrees F and the time to 13 minutes.
8. Select the "MATCH" button to copy the settings for Zone 2.
9. Initiate cooking by pressing the START/STOP button.
10. Flip the patties in the drawers once cooked halfway through.
11. Serve warm and fresh.

Nutrition:
- (Per serving) Calories 305 | Fat 25g | Sodium 532mg | Carbs 2.3g | Fiber 0.4g | Sugar 2g | Protein 18.3g

Puff Pastry

Servings: 6
Cooking Time: 10 Minutes
Ingredients:
- 1 package (200g) cream cheese, softened
- 50g sugar
- 2 tablespoons plain flour
- ½ teaspoon vanilla extract
- 2 large egg yolks
- 1 tablespoon water
- 1 package frozen puff pastry, thawed
- 210g seedless raspberry jam

Directions:
1. Mix the cream cheese, sugar, flour, and vanilla extract until smooth, then add 1 egg yolk.
2. Combine the remaining egg yolk with the water. Unfold each sheet of puff pastry on a lightly floured board and roll into a 30 cm square. Cut into nine 10 cm squares.
3. Put 1 tablespoon cream cheese mixture and 1 rounded teaspoon jam on each. Bring 2 opposite corners of pastry over filling, sealing with yolk mixture.
4. Brush the remaining yolk mixture over the tops.
5. Press your chosen zone - "Zone 1" or "Zone 2" and then rotate the knob to select "Air Fry".
6. Set the temperature to 160 degrees C, and then set the time for 5 minutes to preheat.
7. After preheating, spray the Air-Fryer basket of each zone with cooking spray, line them with parchment paper, and place the pastry on them.
8. Slide the basket into the Air Fryer and set the time for 10 minutes.
9. After cooking time is completed, transfer them onto serving plates and serve.

Cinnamon Air Fryer Apples

Servings: 4
Cooking Time: 15 Minutes
Ingredients:
- 2 apples, cut in half and cored
- 2 tablespoons butter, melted
- 40g oats
- 3 teaspoons honey
- ½ teaspoon ground cinnamon

Directions:
1. Apply the butter to the apple halves' tops.
2. Combine the remaining butter, oats, honey, and cinnamon in a mixing bowl.
3. Distribute the mixture evenly over the apples' tops.
4. Press either "Zone 1" or "Zone 2" and then rotate the knob to select "Air Fryer".
5. Set the temperature to 190 degrees C, and then set the time for 3 minutes to preheat.
6. After preheating, Arrange the apples in the basket.
7. Slide basket into Air Fryer and set the time for 15 minutes.
8. After cooking time is completed, remove basket from Air Fryer.
9. Place them on serving plates and serve.

Parmesan Ranch Risotto And Oat And Chia Porridge

Servings: 6
Cooking Time: 30 Minutes
Ingredients:
- Parmesan Ranch Risotto:
- 1 tablespoon olive oil
- 1 clove garlic, minced
- 1 tablespoon unsalted butter
- 1 onion, diced
- 180 ml Arborio rice
- 475 ml chicken stock, boiling
- 120 ml Parmesan cheese, grated
- Oat and Chia Porridge:
- 2 tablespoons peanut butter
- 4 tablespoons honey
- 1 tablespoon butter, melted
- 1 L milk
- 475 ml oats
- 235 ml chia seeds

Directions:
1. Make the Parmesan Ranch Risotto :
2. Preheat the air fryer to 200°C.
3. Grease a round baking tin with olive oil and stir in the garlic, butter, and onion.
4. Transfer the tin to the zone 1 air fryer basket and bake for 4 minutes. Add the rice and bake for 4 more minutes.
5. Turn the air fryer to 160°C and pour in the chicken stock. Cover and bake for 22 minutes.
6. Scatter with cheese and serve.
7. Make the Oat and Chia Porridge :
8. Preheat the air fryer to 200°C.
9. Put the peanut butter, honey, butter, and milk in a bowl and stir to mix. Add the oats and chia seeds and stir.
10. Transfer the mixture to a bowl and bake in the zone 2 air fryer basket for 5 minutes. Give another stir before serving.

Breakfast Meatballs

Servings: 18 Meatballs
Cooking Time: 15 Minutes
Ingredients:
- 450 g pork sausage meat, removed from casings
- ½ teaspoon salt
- ¼ teaspoon ground black pepper
- 120 ml shredded sharp Cheddar cheese
- 30 g cream cheese, softened
- 1 large egg, whisked

Directions:
1. Combine all ingredients in a large bowl. Form mixture into eighteen 1-inch meatballs.
2. Place meatballs into the two ungreased air fryer drawers. Adjust the temperature to 204°C and air fry for 15 minutes, shaking drawers three times during cooking. Meatballs will be browned on the outside and have an internal temperature of at least 64°C when completely cooked. Serve warm.

Breakfast Stuffed Peppers

Servings: 4
Cooking Time: 13 Minutes
Ingredients:
- 2 capsicums, halved, seeds removed
- 4 eggs
- 1 teaspoon olive oil
- 1 pinch salt and pepper
- 1 pinch sriracha flakes

Directions:
1. Cut each capsicum in half and place two halves in each air fryer basket.
2. Crack one egg into each capsicum and top it with black pepper, salt, sriracha flakes and olive oil.
3. Return the air fryer basket 1 to Zone 1, and basket 2 to Zone 2 of the Ninja Foodi 2-Basket Air Fryer.
4. Choose the "Air Fry" mode for Zone 1 at 390 degrees F and 13 minutes of cooking time.
5. Select the "MATCH COOK" option to copy the settings for Zone 2.
6. Initiate cooking by pressing the START/PAUSE BUTTON.
7. Serve warm.

Nutrition:
- (Per serving) Calories 237 | Fat 19g |Sodium 518mg | Carbs 7g | Fiber 1.5g | Sugar 3.4g | Protein 12g

Pumpkin French Toast Casserole With Sweet And Spicy Twisted Bacon

Servings:4
Cooking Time: 35 Minutes
Ingredients:
- FOR THE FRENCH TOAST CASSEROLE
- 3 large eggs
- 1 cup unsweetened almond milk
- 1 cup canned unsweetened pumpkin puree
- 2 teaspoons pumpkin pie spice
- ¼ cup packed light brown sugar
- 1 teaspoon vanilla extract
- 6 cups French bread cubes
- 1 teaspoon vegetable oil
- ¼ cup maple syrup
- FOR THE BACON
- 2 tablespoons light brown sugar
- ⅛ teaspoon cayenne pepper
- 8 slices bacon

Directions:
1. To prep the French toast casserole: In a shallow bowl, whisk together the eggs, almond milk, pumpkin puree, pumpkin pie spice, brown sugar, and vanilla.
2. Add the bread cubes to the egg mixture, making sure the bread is fully coated in the custard. Let sit for at least 10 minutes to allow the bread to soak up the custard.
3. To prep the bacon: In a small bowl, combine the brown sugar and cayenne.
4. Arrange the bacon on a cutting board in a single layer. Evenly sprinkle the strips with the brown sugar mixture. Fold the bacon strip in half lengthwise. Hold one end of the bacon steady and twist the other end so the bacon resembles a straw.
5. To cook the casserole and bacon: Brush the Zone 1 basket with the oil. Pour the French toast casserole into the Zone 1 basket, drizzle with maple syrup, and insert the basket in the unit. Install a crisper plate in the Zone 2 basket, add the bacon twists in a single layer, and insert the basket in the unit. For the best fit, arrange the bacon twists across the unit, front to back.
6. Select Zone 1, select BAKE, set the temperature to 330°F, and set the time to 35 minutes.
7. Select Zone 2, select AIR FRY, set the temperature to 400°F, and set the time to 12 minutes. Select SMART FINISH.
8. Press START/PAUSE to begin cooking.
9. When cooking is complete, transfer the bacon to a plate lined with paper towels. Let cool for 2 to 3 minutes before serving with the French toast casserole.

Nutrition:
- (Per serving) Calories: 601; Total fat: 28g; Saturated fat: 9g; Carbohydrates: 67g; Fiber: 2.5g; Protein: 17g; Sodium: 814mg

Fish And Seafood Recipes

Chili Honey Salmon

Servings: 2
Cooking Time: 12 Minutes
Ingredients:
- 2 salmon fillets
- 3 tbsp honey
- 1/2 tbsp chili flakes
- 1/2 tsp chili powder
- 1/2 tsp turmeric
- 1 tsp ground coriander
- 1/8 tsp pepper
- 1/8 tsp salt

Directions:
1. Add honey to microwave-safe bowl and heat for 10 seconds.
2. Add chili flakes, chili powder, turmeric, coriander, pepper, and salt into the honey and mix well.
3. Brush salmon fillets with honey mixture.
4. Place salmon fillets into the air fryer basket and cook at 400 F for 12 minutes.
5. Serve and enjoy.

Fried Prawns

Servings: 4
Cooking Time: 5 Minutes
Ingredients:
- 70 g self-raising flour
- 1 teaspoon paprika
- 1 teaspoon salt
- ½ teaspoon freshly ground black pepper
- 1 large egg, beaten
- 120 g finely crushed panko bread crumbs
- 20 frozen large prawns (about 900 g), peeled and deveined
- Cooking spray

Directions:
1. In a shallow bowl, whisk the flour, paprika, salt, and pepper until blended. Add the beaten egg to a second shallow bowl and the bread crumbs to a third.
2. One at a time, dip the prawns into the flour, the egg, and the bread crumbs, coating thoroughly.
3. Preheat the air fryer to 205°C. Line the two air fryer baskets with baking paper.
4. Place the prawns on the baking paper and spritz with oil.
5. Air fry for 2 minutes. Shake the baskets, spritz the prawns with oil, and air fry for 3 minutes more until lightly browned and crispy. Serve hot.

Tuna-stuffed Quinoa Patties

Servings: 4
Cooking Time: 15 Minutes
Ingredients:
- 35 g quinoa
- 4 slices white bread with crusts removed
- 120 ml milk
- 3 eggs
- 280 g tuna packed in olive oil, drained
- 2 to 3 lemons
- Kosher or coarse sea salt, and pepper, to taste
- 150 g panko bread crumbs
- Vegetable oil, for spraying
- Lemon wedges, for serving

Directions:
1. Rinse the quinoa in a fine-mesh sieve until the water runs clear. Bring 1 liter of salted water to a boil. Add the quinoa, cover, and reduce heat to low. Simmer the quinoa covered until most of the water is absorbed and the quinoa is tender, 15 to 20 minutes. Drain and allow to cool to room temperature. Meanwhile, soak the bread in the milk.
2. Mix the drained quinoa with the soaked bread and 2 of the eggs in a large bowl and mix thoroughly. In a medium bowl, combine the tuna, the remaining egg, and the juice and zest of 1 of the lemons. Season well with salt and pepper. Spread the panko on a plate.
3. Scoop up approximately 60 g of the quinoa mixture and flatten into a patty. Place a heaping tablespoon of the tuna mixture in the center of the patty and close the quinoa around the tuna. Flatten the patty slightly to create an oval-shaped croquette. Dredge both sides of the croquette in the panko. Repeat with the remaining quinoa and tuna.
4. Spray the two air fryer baskets with oil to prevent sticking, and preheat the air fryer to 205°C. Arrange 4 or 5 of the croquettes in each basket, taking care to avoid overcrowding. Spray the tops of the croquettes with oil. Air fry for 8 minutes until the top side is browned and crispy. Carefully turn the croquettes over and spray the second side with oil. Air fry until the second side is browned and crispy, another 7 minutes.
5. Serve the croquetas warm with plenty of lemon wedges for spritzing.

Bang Bang Shrimp With Roasted Bok Choy

Servings: 4
Cooking Time: 13 Minutes
Ingredients:
- FOR THE BANG BANG SHRIMP
- ½ cup all-purpose flour
- 2 large eggs
- 1 cup panko bread crumbs
- 1 pound peeled shrimp (tails removed), thawed if frozen
- Nonstick cooking spray
- ½ cup mayonnaise
- ¼ cup Thai sweet chili sauce
- ¼ teaspoon sriracha
- FOR THE BOK CHOY
- 1 tablespoon reduced-sodium soy sauce
- 1 teaspoon minced garlic
- 1 teaspoon sesame oil
- 1 teaspoon minced fresh ginger
- 1½ pounds baby bok choy, halved lengthwise
- 1 tablespoon toasted sesame seeds

Directions:
1. To prep the shrimp: Set up a breading station with three small shallow bowls. Place the flour in the first bowl. In the second bowl, whisk the eggs. Place the panko in the third bowl.
2. Bread the shrimp in this order: First, dip them into the flour, coating both sides. Then, dip into the beaten egg. Finally, coat them in the panko, gently pressing the bread crumbs to adhere to the shrimp. Spritz both sides of the shrimp with cooking spray.
3. To prep the bok choy: In a small bowl, whisk together the soy sauce, garlic, sesame oil, and ginger.
4. To cook the shrimp and bok choy: Install a crisper plate in the Zone 1 basket. Place the shrimp in the basket in a single layer and insert the basket in the unit. Place the boy choy cut-side up in the Zone 2 basket. Pour the sauce over the bok choy and insert the basket in the unit.
5. Select Zone 1, select AIR FRY, set the temperature to 390°F, and set the timer to 13 minutes.
6. Select Zone 2, select BAKE, set the temperature to 370°F, and set the timer to 8 minutes. Select SMART FINISH.
7. Press START/PAUSE to begin cooking.
8. When cooking is complete, the shrimp should be cooked through and golden brown and the bok choy soft and slightly caramelized.
9. In a large bowl, whisk together the mayonnaise, sweet chili sauce, and sriracha. Add the shrimp and toss to coat.
10. Sprinkle the bok choy with the sesame seeds and serve hot alongside the shrimp.

Nutrition:
- (Per serving) Calories: 534; Total fat: 33g; Saturated fat: 4g; Carbohydrates: 29g; Fiber: 3g; Protein: 31g; Sodium: 789mg

Bacon-wrapped Shrimp

Servings: 8
Cooking Time: 10 Minutes
Ingredients:
- 24 jumbo raw shrimp, deveined with tail on, fresh or thawed from frozen
- 8 slices bacon, cut into thirds
- 1 tablespoon olive oil
- 1 teaspoon paprika
- 1–2 cloves minced garlic
- 1 tablespoon finely chopped fresh parsley

Directions:
1. Combine the olive oil, paprika, garlic, and parsley in a small bowl.
2. If necessary, peel the raw shrimp, leaving the tails on.
3. Add the shrimp to the oil mixture. Toss to coat well.
4. Wrap a piece of bacon around the middle of each shrimp and place seam-side down on a small baking dish.
5. Refrigerate for 30 minutes before cooking.
6. Place a crisper plate in each drawer. Put the shrimp in a single layer in each drawer. Insert the drawers into the unit.
7. Select zone 1, then AIR FRY, then set the temperature to 360 degrees F/ 180 degrees C with a 10-minute timer. To match zone 2 settings to zone 1, choose MATCH. To begin, select START/STOP.
8. Remove the shrimp from the drawers when the cooking time is over.

Nutrition:
- (Per serving) Calories 479 | Fat 15.7g | Sodium 949mg | Carbs 0.6g | Fiber 0.1g | Sugar 0g | Protein 76.1g

Miso Salmon And Oyster Po'boy

Servings: 6
Cooking Time: 12 Minutes
Ingredients:
- Miso Salmon:
- 2 tablespoons brown sugar
- 2 tablespoons soy sauce
- 2 tablespoons white miso paste
- 1 teaspoon minced garlic
- 1 teaspoon minced fresh ginger
- ½ teaspoon freshly cracked black pepper
- 2 salmon fillets, 140 g each
- Vegetable oil spray
- 1 teaspoon sesame seeds
- 2 spring onions, thinly sliced, for garnish
- Oyster Po'Boy:
- 105 g plain flour
- 40 g yellow cornmeal
- 1 tablespoon Cajun seasoning
- 1 teaspoon salt
- 2 large eggs, beaten
- 1 teaspoon hot sauce
- 455 g pre-shucked oysters
- 1 (12-inch) French baguette, quartered and sliced horizontally
- Tartar Sauce, as needed
- 150 g shredded lettuce, divided
- 2 tomatoes, cut into slices
- Cooking spray

Directions:
1. Make the Miso Salmon :
2. In a small bowl, whisk together the brown sugar, soy sauce, miso, garlic, ginger, and pepper to combine.
3. Place the salmon fillets on a plate. Pour half the sauce over the fillets; turn the fillets to coat the other sides with sauce.
4. Spray the zone 1 air fryer basket with vegetable oil spray. Place the sauce-covered salmon in the basket. Set the air fryer to 205°C for 12 minutes. Halfway through the cooking time, brush additional miso sauce on the salmon.
5. Sprinkle the salmon with the sesame seeds and spring onions and serve.
6. Make the Oyster Po'Boy :
7. In a shallow bowl, whisk the flour, cornmeal, Cajun seasoning, and salt until blended. In a second shallow bowl, whisk together the eggs and hot sauce.
8. One at a time, dip the oysters in the cornmeal mixture, the eggs, and again in the cornmeal, coating thoroughly.
9. Preheat the air fryer to 205°C. Line the zone 2 air fryer basket with baking paper.
10. Place the oysters on the baking paper and spritz with oil.
11. Air fry for 2 minutes. Shake the basket, spritz the oysters with oil, and air fry for 3 minutes more until lightly browned and crispy.
12. Spread each sandwich half with Tartar Sauce. Assemble the po'boys by layering each sandwich with fried oysters, ½ cup shredded lettuce, and 2 tomato slices.
13. Serve immediately.

Honey Pecan Shrimp

Servings: 4
Cooking Time: 10 Minutes
Ingredients:
- ¼ cup cornstarch
- ¾ teaspoon salt
- ¼ teaspoon black pepper
- 2 egg whites
- ⅔ cup pecans, chopped
- 455g shrimp, peeled, and deveined
- ¼ cup honey
- 2 tablespoons mayonnaise

Directions:
1. Mix cornstarch with ½ teaspoon black pepper, and ½ teaspoon salt in a bowl.
2. Mix pecans and ¼ teaspoon salt in another bowl.
3. Beat egg whites in another bowl.
4. Dredge the shrimp through the cornstarch mixture then dip in the egg whites.
5. Coat the shrimp with pecans mixture.
6. Divide the coated shrimp in the air fryer baskets.
7. Return the air fryer basket 1 to Zone 1, and basket 2 to Zone 2 of the Ninja Foodi 2-Basket Air Fryer.
8. Choose the "Air Fry" mode for Zone 1 at 330 degrees F and 10 minutes of cooking time.
9. Select the "MATCH COOK" option to copy the settings for Zone 2.
10. Initiate cooking by pressing the START/PAUSE BUTTON.
11. Flip the shrimps once cooked halfway through.
12. Serve.

Nutrition:
- (Per serving) Calories 155 | Fat 4.2g |Sodium 963mg | Carbs 21.5g | Fiber 0.8g | Sugar 5.7g | Protein 8.1g

Basil Cheese Salmon

Servings: 4
Cooking Time: 7 Minutes
Ingredients:
- 4 salmon fillets
- 1/4 cup parmesan cheese, grated
- 5 fresh basil leaves, minced
- 2 tbsp mayonnaise
- 1/2 lemon juice
- Pepper
- Salt

Directions:
1. Preheat the air fryer to 400 F.
2. Brush salmon fillets with lemon juice and season with pepper and salt.
3. In a small bowl, mix mayonnaise, basil, and cheese.
4. Spray air fryer basket with cooking spray.
5. Place salmon fillets into the air fryer basket and brush with mayonnaise mixture and cook for 7 minutes.
6. Serve and enjoy.

Keto Baked Salmon With Pesto

Servings: 2
Cooking Time: 18
Ingredients:
- 4 salmon fillets, 2 inches thick
- 2 ounces green pesto
- Salt and black pepper
- ½ tablespoon of canola oil, for greasing
- 1-1/2 cup mayonnaise
- 2 tablespoons Greek yogurt
- Salt and black pepper, to taste

Directions:
1. Rub the salmon with pesto, salt, oil, and black pepper.
2. In a small bowl, whisk together all the green sauce ingredients.
3. Divide the fish fillets between both the baskets.
4. Set zone 1 to air fry mode for 18 minutes at 390 degrees F.
5. Select MATCH button for Zone 2 basket.
6. Once the cooking is done, serve it with green sauce drizzle.
7. Enjoy.

Nutrition:
- (Per serving) Calories 1165 | Fat 80.7 g | Sodium 1087 mg | Carbs 33.1g | Fiber 0.5g | Sugar 11.5 g | Protein 80.6g

Rainbow Salmon Kebabs And Tuna Melt

Servings: 3
Cooking Time: 10 Minutes
Ingredients:
- Rainbow Salmon Kebabs:
- 170 g boneless, skinless salmon, cut into 1-inch cubes
- ¼ medium red onion, peeled and cut into 1-inch pieces
- ½ medium yellow bell pepper, seeded and cut into 1-inch pieces
- ½ medium courgette, trimmed and cut into ½-inch slices
- 1 tablespoon olive oil
- ½ teaspoon salt
- ¼ teaspoon ground black pepper
- Tuna Melt:
- Olive or vegetable oil, for spraying
- 140 g can tuna, drained
- 1 tablespoon mayonnaise
- ¼ teaspoon garlic granules, plus more for garnish
- 2 teaspoons unsalted butte
- 2 slices sandwich bread of choice
- 2 slices Cheddar cheese

Directions:
1. Make the Rainbow Salmon Kebabs : Using one skewer, skewer 1 piece salmon, then 1 piece onion, 1 piece bell pepper, and finally 1 piece courgette. Repeat this pattern with additional skewers to make four kebabs total. Drizzle with olive oil and sprinkle with salt and black pepper. 2. Place kebabs into the ungreased zone 1 air fryer drawer. Adjust the temperature to 204°C and air fry for 8 minutes, turning kebabs halfway through cooking. Salmon will easily flake and have an internal temperature of at least 64°C when done; vegetables will be tender. Serve warm.
2. Make the Tuna Melt : 1. Line the zone 2 air fryer drawer with baking paper and spray lightly with oil. In a medium bowl, mix together the tuna, mayonnaise, and garlic. 3. Spread 1 teaspoon of butter on each slice of bread and place one slice butter-side down in the prepared drawer. 4. Top with a slice of cheese, the tuna mixture, another slice of cheese, and the other slice of bread, butter-side up. 5. Air fry at 204°C for 5 minutes, flip, and cook for another 5 minutes, until browned and crispy. 6. Sprinkle with additional garlic, before cutting in half and serving.

Parmesan-crusted Fish Sticks With Baked Macaroni And Cheese

Servings: 4
Cooking Time: 25 Minutes
Ingredients:
- FOR THE FISH STICKS
- 1 pound cod or haddock fillets
- ½ cup all-purpose flour
- 2 large eggs
- ¼ teaspoon kosher salt
- ¼ teaspoon freshly ground black pepper
- ¾ cup panko bread crumbs
- ¼ cup grated Parmesan cheese
- Nonstick cooking spray
- FOR THE MACARONI AND CHEESE
- 1½ cups elbow macaroni
- 1 cup whole milk
- ½ cup heavy (whipping) cream
- 8 ounces shredded Colby-Jack cheese
- 4 ounces cream cheese, at room temperature
- 1 teaspoon Dijon mustard
- ½ teaspoon kosher salt
- ½ teaspoon freshly ground black pepper

Directions:
1. To prep the fish sticks: Cut the fish into sticks about 3 inches long and ¾ inch wide.
2. Set up a breading station with three small shallow bowls. Place the flour in the first bowl. In the second bowl, whisk the eggs and season with the salt and black pepper. Combine the panko and Parmesan in the third bowl.
3. Bread the fish sticks in this order: First, dip them into the flour, coating all sides. Then, dip into the beaten egg. Finally, coat them in the panko mixture, gently pressing the bread crumbs into the fish. Spritz each fish stick all over with cooking spray.
4. To prep the macaroni and cheese: Place the macaroni in the Zone 2 basket. Add the milk, cream, Colby-Jack, cream cheese, mustard, salt, and black pepper. Stir well to combine, ensuring the pasta is completely submerged in the liquid.
5. To cook the fish sticks and macaroni and cheese: Install a crisper plate in the Zone 1 basket. Arrange the fish sticks in a single layer in the basket (use a rack or cook in batches if necessary) and insert the basket in the unit. Insert the Zone 2 basket in the unit.
6. Select Zone 1, select AIR FRY, set the temperature to 390°F, and set the timer to 18 minutes.
7. Select Zone 2, select BAKE, set the temperature to 360°F, and set the timer to 25 minutes. Select SMART FINISH.
8. Press START/PAUSE to begin cooking.
9. When the Zone 1 timer reads 3 minutes, press START/PAUSE. Remove the basket and use silicone-tipped tongs to gently flip over the fish sticks. Reinsert the basket and press START/PAUSE to resume cooking.
10. When cooking is complete, the fish sticks should be crisp and the macaroni tender.
11. Stir the macaroni and cheese and let stand for 5 minutes before serving. The sauce will thicken as it cools.

Nutrition:
- (Per serving) Calories: 903; Total fat: 51g; Saturated fat: 25g; Carbohydrates: 60g; Fiber: 2.5g; Protein: 48g; Sodium: 844mg

Two-way Salmon

Servings: 2
Cooking Time: 18
Ingredients:
- 2 salmon fillets, 8 ounces each
- 2 tablespoons of Cajun seasoning
- 2 tablespoons of jerk seasoning
- 1 lemon cut in half
- oil spray, for greasing

Directions:
1. First, drizzle lemon juice over the salmon and wash it with tap water.
2. Rinse and pat dry the fillets with a paper towel.
3. Now rub o fillet with Cajun seasoning and grease it with oil spray.
4. Take the second fillet and rub it with jerk seasoning.
5. Grease the second fillet of salmon with oil spray.
6. now put the salmon fillets in both the baskets.
7. Set the Zone 1 basket to 390 degrees F for 16-18 minutes
8. Select MATCH button for zone 2 basket.
9. hit the start button to start cooking.
10. Once the cooking is done, serve the fish hot with mayonnaise.

Nutrition:
- (Per serving) Calories 238| Fat 11.8g| Sodium 488mg | Carbs 9g | Fiber 0g | Sugar 8 g | Protein 35g

Cod With Jalapeño

Servings: 4
Cooking Time: 14 Minutes
Ingredients:
- 4 cod fillets, boneless
- 1 jalapeño, minced
- 1 tablespoon avocado oil
- ½ teaspoon minced garlic

Directions:
1. In the shallow bowl, mix minced jalapeño, avocado oil, and minced garlic.
2. Put the cod fillets in the two air fryer drawers in one layer and top with minced jalapeño mixture.
3. Cook the fish at 185°C for 7 minutes per side.

Prawn Creole Casserole And Garlic Lemon Scallops

Servings: 8
Cooking Time: 25 Minutes
Ingredients:
- Prawn Creole Casserole:
- 360 g prawns, peeled and deveined
- 50 g chopped celery
- 50 g chopped onion
- 50 g chopped green bell pepper
- 2 large eggs, beaten
- 240 ml single cream
- 1 tablespoon butter, melted
- 1 tablespoon cornflour
- 1 teaspoon Creole seasoning
- ¾ teaspoon salt
- ½ teaspoon freshly ground black pepper
- 120 g shredded Cheddar cheese
- Cooking spray
- Garlic Lemon Scallops:
- 4 tablespoons salted butter, melted
- 4 teaspoons peeled and finely minced garlic
- ½ small lemon, zested and juiced
- 8 sea scallops, 30 g each, cleaned and patted dry
- ¼ teaspoon salt
- ¼ teaspoon ground black pepper

Directions:
1. Make the Prawn Creole Casserole :
2. In a medium bowl, stir together the prawns, celery, onion, and green pepper.
3. In another medium bowl, whisk the eggs, single cream, butter, cornflour, Creole seasoning, salt, and pepper until blended. Stir the egg mixture into the prawn mixture. Add the cheese and stir to combine.
4. Preheat the air fryer to 150°C. Spritz a baking pan with oil.
5. Transfer the prawn mixture to the prepared pan and place it in the zone 1 air fryer drawer.
6. Bake for 25 minutes, stirring every 10 minutes, until a knife inserted into the center comes out clean.
7. Serve immediately.
8. Make the Garlic Lemon Scallops :
9. In a small bowl, mix butter, garlic, lemon zest, and lemon juice. Place scallops in an ungreased round nonstick baking dish. Pour butter mixture over scallops, then sprinkle with salt and pepper.
10. Place dish into the zone 2 air fryer drawer. Adjust the temperature to 182°C and bake for 10 minutes. Scallops will be opaque and firm, and have an internal temperature of 56°C when done. Serve warm.

Butter-wine Baked Salmon

Servings: 4
Cooking Time: 10 Minutes
Ingredients:
- 4 tablespoons butter, melted
- 2 cloves garlic, minced
- Sea salt and ground black pepper, to taste
- 60 ml dry white wine or apple cider vinegar
- 1 tablespoon lime juice
- 1 teaspoon smoked paprika
- ½ teaspoon onion powder
- 4 salmon steaks
- Cooking spray

Directions:
1. Place all the ingredients except the salmon and oil in a shallow dish and stir to mix well.
2. Add the salmon steaks, turning to coat well on both sides. Transfer the salmon to the refrigerator to marinate for 30 minutes.
3. Preheat the air fryer to 182°C.
4. Place the salmon steaks in the two air fryer drawers, discarding any excess marinade. Spray the salmon steaks with cooking spray.
5. Air fry for about 10 minutes, flipping the salmon steaks halfway through, or until cooked to your preferred doneness.
6. Divide the salmon steaks among four plates and serve.

Basil Cheese S·saltalmon

Servings: 4
Cooking Time: 7 Minutes
Ingredients:
- 4 salmon fillets
- 1/4 cup parmesan cheese, grated
- 5 fresh basil leaves, minced
- 2 tbsp mayonnaise
- 1/2 lemon juice
- Pepper

Directions:
1. Preheat the air fryer to 400 F.
2. Brush salmon fillets with lemon juice and season with pepper and salt.
3. In a small bowl, mix mayonnaise, basil, and cheese.
4. Spray air fryer basket with cooking spray.
5. Place salmon fillets into the air fryer basket and brush with mayonnaise mixture and cook for 7 minutes.
6. Serve and enjoy.

Fried Lobster Tails

Servings: 4
Cooking Time: 18 Minutes
Ingredients:
- 4 (4-oz) lobster tails
- 8 tablespoons butter, melted
- 2 teaspoons lemon zest
- 2 garlic cloves, grated
- Salt and black pepper, ground to taste
- 2 teaspoons fresh parsley, chopped
- 4 wedges lemon

Directions:
1. Spread the lobster tails into Butterfly, slit the top to expose the lobster meat while keeping the tail intact.
2. Place two lobster tails in each of the crisper plate with their lobster meat facing up.
3. Mix melted butter with lemon zest and garlic in a bowl.
4. Brush the butter mixture on top of the lobster tails.
5. And drizzle salt and black pepper on top.
6. Return the crisper plate to the Ninja Foodi Dual Zone Air Fryer.
7. Choose the Air Fry mode for Zone 1 and set the temperature to 390 degrees F and the time to 18 minutes|
8. Select the "MATCH" button to copy the settings for Zone 2.
9. Initiate cooking by pressing the START/STOP button.
10. Garnish with parsley and lemon wedges.
11. Serve warm.

Orange-mustard Glazed Salmon

Servings: 2
Cooking Time: 10 Minutes
Ingredients:
- 1 tablespoon orange marmalade
- ¼ teaspoon grated orange zest plus 1 tablespoon juice
- 2 teaspoons whole-grain mustard
- 2 (230 g) skin-on salmon fillets, 1½ inches thick
- Salt and pepper, to taste
- Vegetable oil spray

Directions:
1. Preheat the zone 1 air fryer drawer to 204°C.
2. Make foil sling for air fryer drawer by folding 1 long sheet of aluminum foil so it is 4 inches wide. Lay sheet of foil widthwise across drawer, pressing foil into and up sides of drawer. Fold excess foil as needed so that edges of foil are flush with top of drawer. Lightly spray foil and drawer with vegetable oil spray.
3. Combine marmalade, orange zest and juice, and mustard in bowl. Pat salmon dry with paper towels and season with salt and pepper. Brush tops and sides of fillets evenly with glaze. Arrange fillets skin side down on sling in prepared drawer, spaced evenly apart. Air fry salmon until center is still translucent when checked with the tip of a paring knife and registers 52°C, 10 to 14 minutes, using sling to rotate fillets halfway through cooking.
4. Using the sling, carefully remove salmon from air fryer. Slide fish spatula along underside of fillets and transfer to individual serving plates, leaving skin behind. Serve.

Thai Prawn Skewers And Lemon-tarragon Fish En Papillote

Servings: 5
Cooking Time: 15 Minutes
Ingredients:
- Lemon-Tarragon Fish en Papillote:
- Salt and pepper, to taste
- 340 g extra-large prawns, peeled and deveined
- 1 tablespoon vegetable oil
- 1 teaspoon honey
- ½ teaspoon grated lime zest plus 1 tablespoon juice, plus lime wedges for serving
- 6 (6-inch) wooden skewers
- 3 tablespoons creamy peanut butter
- 3 tablespoons hot tap water
- 1 tablespoon chopped fresh coriander
- 1 teaspoon fish sauce
- Lemon-Tarragon Fish en Papillote:
- 2 tablespoons salted butter, melted
- 1 tablespoon fresh lemon juice
- ½ teaspoon dried tarragon, crushed, or 2 sprigs fresh tarragon
- 1 teaspoon kosher or coarse sea salt
- 85 g julienned carrots
- 435 g julienned fennel, or 1 stalk julienned celery
- 75 g thinly sliced red bell pepper
- 2 cod fillets, 170 g each, thawed if frozen
- Vegetable oil spray
- ½ teaspoon black pepper

Directions:
1. Make the Lemon-Tarragon Fish en Papillote :
2. Preheat the air fryer to 204°C.
3. Dissolve 2 tablespoons salt in 1 litre cold water in a large container. Add prawns, cover, and refrigerate for 15 minutes.
4. Remove prawns from brine and pat dry with paper towels. Whisk oil, honey, lime zest, and ¼ teaspoon pepper together in a large bowl. Add prawns and toss to coat. Thread prawns onto skewers, leaving about ¼ inch between each prawns .
5. Arrange 3 skewers in the zone 1 air fryer drawer, parallel to each other and spaced evenly apart. Arrange remaining 3 skewers on top, perpendicular to the bottom layer. Air fry until prawns are opaque throughout, 6 to 8 minutes, flipping and rotating skewers halfway through cooking.
6. Whisk peanut butter, hot tap water, lime juice, coriander, and fish sauce together in a bowl until smooth. Serve skewers with peanut dipping sauce and lime wedges.
7. Make the Lemon-Tarragon Fish en Papillote :
8. In a medium bowl, combine the butter, lemon juice, tarragon, and ½ teaspoon of the salt. Whisk well until you get a creamy sauce. Add the carrots, fennel, and bell pepper and toss to combine; set aside.
9. Cut two squares of baking paper each large enough to hold one fillet and half the vegetables. Spray the fillets with vegetable oil spray. Season both sides with the remaining ½ teaspoon salt and the black pepper.
10. Lay one fillet down on each baking paper square. Top each with half the vegetables. Pour any remaining sauce over the vegetables.
11. Fold over the baking paper and crimp the sides in small, tight folds to hold the fish, vegetables, and sauce securely inside the packet. Place the packets in the zone 2 air fryer drawer. Set the air fryer to 176°C for 15 minutes.
12. Transfer each packet to a plate. Cut open with scissors just before serving .

Lemon Pepper Fish Fillets

Servings: 4
Cooking Time: 10 Minutes
Ingredients:
- 4 tilapia fillets
- 30ml olive oil
- 2 tbsp lemon zest
- ⅛ tsp paprika
- 1 tsp garlic, minced
- 1 ½ tsp ground peppercorns
- Pepper
- Salt

Directions:
1. In a small bowl, mix oil, peppercorns, paprika, garlic, lemon zest, pepper, and salt.
2. Brush the fish fillets with oil mixture.
3. Insert a crisper plate in the Ninja Foodi air fryer baskets.
4. Place fish fillets in both baskets.
5. Select zone 1 then select "air fry" mode and set the temperature to 390 degrees F for 10 minutes. Press "match" to match zone 2 settings to zone 1. Press "start/stop" to begin.

Nutrition:
- (Per serving) Calories 203 | Fat 9g |Sodium 99mg | Carbs 0.9g | Fiber 0.2g | Sugar 0.2g | Protein 32.1g

Perfect Parmesan Salmon

Servings: 4
Cooking Time: 10 Minutes
Ingredients:
- 4 salmon fillets
- 1/4 cup parmesan cheese, shredded
- 1/4 tsp dried dill
- 1/2 tbsp Dijon mustard
- 4 tbsp mayonnaise
- 1 lemon juice
- Pepper
- Salt

Directions:
1. In a small bowl, mix cheese, dill, mustard, mayonnaise, lemon juice, pepper, and salt.
2. Place salmon fillets into the air fryer basket and brush with cheese mixture.
3. Cook salmon fillets at 400 F for 10 minutes.
4. Serve and enjoy.

Tandoori Prawns

Servings: 4
Cooking Time: 6 Minutes
Ingredients:
- 455 g jumbo raw prawns (21 to 25 count), peeled and deveined
- 1 tablespoon minced fresh ginger
- 3 cloves garlic, minced
- 5 g chopped fresh coriander or parsley, plus more for garnish
- 1 teaspoon ground turmeric
- 1 teaspoon garam masala
- 1 teaspoon smoked paprika
- 1 teaspoon kosher or coarse sea salt
- ½ to 1 teaspoon cayenne pepper
- 2 tablespoons olive oil (for Paleo) or melted ghee
- 2 teaspoons fresh lemon juice

Directions:
1. In a large bowl, combine the prawns, ginger, garlic, coriander, turmeric, garam masala, paprika, salt, and cayenne. Toss well to coat. Add the oil or ghee and toss again. Marinate at room temperature for 15 minutes, or cover and refrigerate for up to 8 hours.
2. Place the prawns in a single layer in the two air fryer baskets. Set the air fryer to 165°C for 6 minutes. Transfer the prawns to a serving platter. Cover and let the prawns finish cooking in the residual heat, about 5 minutes.
3. Sprinkle the prawns with the lemon juice and toss to coat. Garnish with additional cilantro and serve.

Dukkah-crusted Halibut

Servings: 2
Cooking Time: 17 Minutes
Ingredients:
- Dukkah:
- 1 tablespoon coriander seeds
- 1 tablespoon sesame seeds
- 1½ teaspoons cumin seeds
- 50 g roasted mixed nuts
- ¼ teaspoon kosher or coarse sea salt
- ¼ teaspoon black pepper
- Fish:
- 2 halibut fillets, 140 g each
- 2 tablespoons mayonnaise
- Vegetable oil spray
- Lemon wedges, for serving

Directions:
1. For the Dukkah: Combine the coriander, sesame seeds, and cumin in a small baking pan. Place the pan in the zone 1 air fryer basket. Set the air fryer to 205°C for 5 minutes. Toward the end of the cooking time, you will hear the seeds popping. Transfer to a plate and let cool for 5 minutes. 2. Transfer the toasted seeds to a food processor or spice grinder and add the mixed nuts. Pulse until coarsely chopped. Add the salt and pepper and stir well.
2. 3. For the fish: Spread each fillet with 1 tablespoon of the mayonnaise. Press a heaping tablespoon of the Dukkah into the mayonnaise on each fillet, pressing lightly to adhere. 4. Spray the zone 2 air fryer basket with vegetable oil spray. Place the fish in the zone 2 basket. Cook for 12 minutes, or until the fish flakes easily with a fork. 5. Serve the fish with lemon wedges.

Savory Salmon Fillets

Servings: 4
Cooking Time: 17 Minutes
Ingredients:
- 4 (6-oz) salmon fillets
- Salt, to taste
- Black pepper, to taste
- 4 teaspoons olive oil
- 4 tablespoons wholegrain mustard
- 2 tablespoons packed brown sugar
- 2 garlic cloves, minced
- 1 teaspoon thyme leaves

Directions:
1. Rub the salmon with salt and black pepper first.
2. Whisk oil with sugar, thyme, garlic, and mustard in a small bowl.
3. Place two salmon fillets in each of the crisper plate and brush the thyme mixture on top of each fillet.
4. Return the crisper plates to the Ninja Foodi Dual Zone Air Fryer.
5. Choose the Air Fry mode for Zone 1 and set the temperature to 390 degrees F and the time to 17 minutes|
6. Select the "MATCH" button to copy the settings for Zone 2.
7. Initiate cooking by pressing the START/STOP button.
8. Serve warm and fresh.

Fried Tilapia

Servings: 4
Cooking Time: 20 Minutes
Ingredients:
- 4 fresh tilapia fillets, approximately 6 ounces each
- 2 teaspoons olive oil
- 2 teaspoons chopped fresh chives
- 2 teaspoons chopped fresh parsley
- 1 teaspoon minced garlic
- Freshly ground pepper, to taste
- Salt to taste

Directions:
1. Pat the tilapia fillets dry with a paper towel.
2. Stir together the olive oil, chives, parsley, garlic, salt, and pepper in a small bowl.
3. Brush the mixture over the top of the tilapia fillets.
4. Place a crisper plate in each drawer. Add the fillets in a single layer to each drawer. Insert the drawers into the unit.
5. Select zone 1, then AIR FRY, then set the temperature to 360 degrees F/ 180 degrees C with a 20-minute timer. To match zone 2 settings to zone 1, choose MATCH. To begin, select START/STOP.
6. Remove the tilapia fillets from the drawers after the timer has finished.

Nutrition:
- (Per serving) Calories 140 | Fat 5.7g | Sodium 125mg | Carbs 1.5g | Fiber 0.4g | Sugar 0g | Protein 21.7g

Panko-crusted Fish Sticks

Servings: 4
Cooking Time: 15 Minutes
Ingredients:
- Tartar Sauce:
- 470 ml mayonnaise
- 2 tablespoons dill pickle relish
- 1 tablespoon dried minced onions
- Fish Sticks:
- Olive or vegetable oil, for spraying
- 455 g tilapia fillets
- 75 g plain flour
- 120 g panko bread crumbs
- 2 tablespoons Creole seasoning
- 2 teaspoons garlic granules
- 1 teaspoon onion powder
- ½ teaspoon salt
- ¼ teaspoon freshly ground black pepper
- 1 large egg

Directions:
1. Make the Tartar Sauce: In a small bowl, whisk together the mayonnaise, pickle relish, and onions. Cover with plastic wrap and refrigerate until ready to serve. You can make this sauce ahead of time; the flavors will intensify as it chills. Make the Fish Sticks: 2. Preheat the air fryer to 175°C. Line the two air fryer baskets with baking paper and spray lightly with oil. 3. Cut the fillets into equal-size sticks and place them in a zip-top plastic bag. 4. Add the flour to the bag, seal, and shake well until evenly coated. 5. In a shallow bowl, mix together the bread crumbs, Creole seasoning, garlic, onion powder, salt, and black pepper. 6. In a small bowl, whisk the egg. 7. Dip the fish sticks in the egg, then dredge in the bread crumb mixture until completely coated. 8. Place the fish sticks in the two prepared baskets. Do not overcrowd. Spray lightly with oil. 9. Cook for 12 to 15 minutes, or until browned and cooked through. Serve with the tartar sauce.

Broiled Crab Cakes With Hush Puppies

Servings: 4
Cooking Time: 15 Minutes
Ingredients:
- FOR THE CRAB CAKES
- 2 large eggs
- 2 tablespoons Dijon mustard
- 2 teaspoons Worcestershire sauce
- 1 teaspoon Old Bay seasoning
- ¼ teaspoon paprika
- ¼ cup cracker crumbs (about 9 crackers)
- 1 pound lump crab meat
- 2 teaspoons vegetable oil
- FOR THE HUSH PUPPIES
- ½ cup all-purpose flour
- ⅓ cup yellow cornmeal
- 3 tablespoons sugar
- ¼ teaspoon kosher salt
- ¼ teaspoon baking powder
- 1 large egg
- ½ cup whole milk
- Nonstick cooking spray

Directions:
1. To prep the crab cakes: In a large bowl, whisk together the eggs, mustard, Worcestershire, Old Bay, and paprika until smooth. Stir in the cracker crumbs until fully incorporated, then fold in the crab meat. Refrigerate the crab mixture for 30 minutes.
2. Divide the crab mixture into 8 equal portions. With damp hands, press each portion gently into a loose patty. Brush both sides of each patty with the oil.
3. To prep the hush puppies: In a large bowl, combine the flour, cornmeal, sugar, salt, and baking powder. Stir in the egg and milk to form a stiff batter.
4. Roll the batter into 8 balls. Spritz each hush puppy with cooking spray.
5. To cook the crab cakes and hush puppies: Install a crisper plate in each of the two baskets. Place the crab cakes in a single layer in the Zone 1 basket and insert the basket in the unit. Line the Zone 2 plate with aluminum foil and spray the foil with cooking spray. Arrange the hush puppies on the foil and insert the basket in the unit.
6. Select Zone 1, select AIR BROIL, set the temperature to 400°F, and set the timer to 15 minutes.
7. Select Zone 2, select AIR FRY, set the temperature to 400°F, and set the timer to 7 minutes. Select SMART FINISH.
8. Press START/PAUSE to begin cooking.
9. When cooking is complete, the crab cakes and hush puppies will be golden brown and cooked through. Serve hot.

Nutrition:
- (Per serving) Calories: 403; Total fat: 16g; Saturated fat: 2g; Carbohydrates: 40g; Fiber: 1g; Protein: 27g; Sodium: 872mg

Classic Fish Sticks With Tartar Sauce

Servings: 4
Cooking Time: 12 To 15 Minutes
Ingredients:
- 680 g cod fillets, cut into 1-inch strips
- 1 teaspoon salt
- ½ teaspoon freshly ground black pepper
- 2 eggs
- 70 g almond flour
- 20 g grated Parmesan cheese
- Tartar Sauce:
- 120 ml sour cream
- 120 ml mayonnaise
- 3 tablespoons chopped dill pickle
- 2 tablespoons capers, drained and chopped
- ½ teaspoon dried dill
- 1 tablespoon dill pickle liquid (optional)

Directions:
1. Preheat the air fryer to 204°C. 2. Season the cod with the salt and black pepper; set aside. 3. In a shallow bowl, lightly beat the eggs. In a second shallow bowl, combine the almond flour and Parmesan cheese. Stir until thoroughly combined. 4. Working with a few pieces at a time, dip the fish into the egg mixture followed by the flour mixture. Press lightly to ensure an even coating. 5. Arrange the fish in a single layer in the two air fryer drawers and spray lightly with olive oil. Pausing halfway through the cooking time to turn the fish, air fry for 12 to 15 minutes, until the fish flakes easily with a fork. Let sit in the drawer for a few minutes before serving with the tartar sauce. 6. To make the tartar sauce: In a small bowl, combine the sour cream, mayonnaise, pickle, capers, and dill. If you prefer a thinner sauce, stir in the pickle liquid.

Frozen Breaded Fish Fillet

Servings: 2
Cooking Time: 12
Ingredients:
- 4 Frozen Breaded Fish Fillet
- Oil spray, for greasing
- 1 cup mayonnaise

Directions:
1. Take the frozen fish fillets out of the bag and place them in both baskets of the air fryer.
2. Lightly grease it with oil spray.
3. Set the Zone 1 basket to 380 degrees F fo12 minutes.
4. Select the MATCH button for the zone 2 basket.
5. hit the start button to start cooking.
6. Once the cooking is done, serve the fish hot with mayonnaise.

Nutrition:
- (Per serving) Calories 921| Fat 61.5g| Sodium 1575mg | Carbs 69g | Fiber 2g | Sugar 9.5g | Protein 29.1g

Crustless Prawn Quiche

Servings: 2
Cooking Time: 20 Minutes
Ingredients:
- Vegetable oil
- 4 large eggs
- 120 ml single cream
- 110 g raw prawns, chopped
- 120 g shredded Parmesan or Swiss cheese
- 235 g chopped spring onions
- 1 teaspoon sweet smoked paprika
- 1 teaspoon Herbes de Provence
- 1 teaspoon black pepper
- ½ to 1 teaspoon kosher or coarse sea salt

Directions:
1. Generously grease a baking pan with vegetable oil.
2. In a large bowl, beat together the eggs and single cream. Add the prawns, 90 g of the cheese, the scallions, paprika, Herbes de Provence, pepper, and salt. Stir with a fork to thoroughly combine. Pour the egg mixture into the prepared pan.
3. Place the pan in the zone 1 air fryer basket. Set the air fryer to 150°C for 20 minutes. After 17 minutes, sprinkle the remaining 30 g cheese on top and cook for the remaining 3 minutes, or until the cheese has melted, the eggs are set, and a toothpick inserted into the center comes out clean.
4. Serve the quiche warm or at room temperature.

Roasted Salmon Fillets & Chilli Lime Prawns

Servings: 6
Cooking Time: 10 Minutes
Ingredients:
- Roasted Salmon Fillets:
- 2 (230 g) skin-on salmon fillets, 1½ inches thick
- 1 teaspoon vegetable oil
- Salt and pepper, to taste
- Vegetable oil spray
- Chilli Lime Prawns:
- 455 g medium prawns, peeled and deveined
- 1 tablespoon salted butter, melted
- 2 teaspoons chilli powder
- ¼ teaspoon garlic powder
- ¼ teaspoon salt
- ¼ teaspoon ground black pepper
- ½ small lime, zested and juiced, divided

Directions:
1. Make the Roasted Salmon Fillets :
2. Preheat the air fryer to 205°C.
3. Make foil sling for air fryer basket by folding 1 long sheet of aluminum foil so it is 4 inches wide. Lay sheet of foil widthwise across zone 1 basket, pressing foil into and up sides of basket. Fold excess foil as needed so that edges of foil are flush with top of basket. Lightly spray foil and basket with vegetable oil spray.
4. Pat salmon dry with paper towels, rub with oil, and season with salt and pepper. Arrange fillets skin side down on sling in prepared zone 1 basket, spaced evenly apart. Air fry salmon until center is still translucent when checked with the tip of a paring knife and registers 50°C , 10 to 14 minutes, using sling to rotate fillets halfway through cooking.
5. Using the sling, carefully remove salmon from air fryer. Slide fish spatula along underside of fillets and transfer to individual serving plates, leaving skin behind. Serve.
6. Make the Chilli Lime Prawns :
7. In a medium bowl, toss prawns with butter, then sprinkle with chilli powder, garlic powder, salt, pepper, and lime zest.
8. Place prawns into ungreased zone 2 air fryer basket. Adjust the temperature to 205°C and air fry for 5 minutes. Prawns will be firm and form a "C" shape when done.
9. Transfer prawns to a large serving dish and drizzle with lime juice. Serve warm.

Blackened Red Snapper

Servings: 4
Cooking Time: 8 To 10 Minutes
Ingredients:
- 1½ teaspoons black pepper
- ¼ teaspoon thyme
- ¼ teaspoon garlic powder
- ⅛ teaspoon cayenne pepper
- 1 teaspoon olive oil
- 4 red snapper fillet portions, skin on, 110 g each
- 4 thin slices lemon
- Cooking spray

Directions:
1. Mix the spices and oil together to make a paste. Rub into both sides of the fish.
2. Spray the two air fryer drawers with nonstick cooking spray and lay snapper steaks in drawers, skin-side down.
3. Place a lemon slice on each piece of fish.
4. Roast at 200°C for 8 to 10 minutes. The fish will not flake when done, but it should be white through the center.

Herbed Prawns Pita

Servings: 4
Cooking Time: 8 Minutes
Ingredients:
- 455 g medium prawns, peeled and deveined
- 2 tablespoons olive oil
- 1 teaspoon dried oregano
- ½ teaspoon dried thyme
- ½ teaspoon garlic powder
- ¼ teaspoon onion powder
- ½ teaspoon salt
- ¼ teaspoon black pepper
- 4 whole wheat pitas
- 110 g feta cheese, crumbled
- 75 g shredded lettuce
- 1 tomato, diced
- 45 g black olives, sliced
- 1 lemon

Directions:
1. Preheat the oven to 192°C.
2. In a medium bowl, combine the prawns with the olive oil, oregano, thyme, garlic powder, onion powder, salt, and black pepper.
3. Pour prawns in a single layer in the two air fryer drawers and roast for 6 to 8 minutes, or until cooked through.
4. Remove from the air fryer and divide into warmed pitas with feta, lettuce, tomato, olives, and a squeeze of lemon.

Steamed Cod With Garlic And Swiss Chard

Servings: 4
Cooking Time: 12 Minutes
Ingredients:
- 1 teaspoon salt
- ½ teaspoon dried oregano
- ½ teaspoon dried thyme
- ½ teaspoon garlic powder
- 4 cod fillets
- ½ white onion, thinly sliced
- 135 g Swiss chard, washed, stemmed, and torn into pieces
- 60 ml olive oil
- 1 lemon, quartered

Directions:
1. Preheat the air fryer to 192°C.
2. In a small bowl, whisk together the salt, oregano, thyme, and garlic powder.
3. Tear off four pieces of aluminum foil, with each sheet being large enough to envelop one cod fillet and a quarter of the vegetables.
4. Place a cod fillet in the middle of each sheet of foil, then sprinkle on all sides with the spice mixture.
5. In each foil packet, place a quarter of the onion slices and 30 g Swiss chard, then drizzle 1 tablespoon olive oil and squeeze ¼ lemon over the contents of each foil packet.
6. Fold and seal the sides of the foil packets and then place them into the two air fryer drawers. Steam for 12 minutes.
7. Remove from the drawers, and carefully open each packet to avoid a steam burn.

Country Prawns

Servings: 4
Cooking Time: 15 To 20 Minutes
Ingredients:
- 455 g large prawns, peeled and deveined, with tails on
- 455 g smoked sausage, cut into thick slices
- 2 corn cobs, quartered
- 1 courgette, cut into bite-sized pieces
- 1 red bell pepper, cut into chunks
- 1 tablespoon Old Bay seasoning
- 2 tablespoons olive oil
- Cooking spray

Directions:
1. Preheat the air fryer to 204°C. Spray the air fryer drawer lightly with cooking spray.
2. In a large bowl, mix the prawns, sausage, corn, courgette, bell pepper, and Old Bay seasoning, and toss to coat with the spices. Add the olive oil and toss again until evenly coated.
3. Spread the mixture in the two air fryer drawers in a single layer.
4. Air fry for 15 to 20 minutes, or until cooked through, shaking the drawers every 5 minutes for even cooking.
5. Serve immediately.

Tuna With Herbs

Servings: 4
Cooking Time: 17 Minutes
Ingredients:
- 1 tablespoon butter, melted
- 1 medium-sized leek, thinly sliced
- 1 tablespoon chicken stock
- 1 tablespoon dry white wine
- 455 g tuna
- ½ teaspoon red pepper flakes, crushed
- Sea salt and ground black pepper, to taste
- ½ teaspoon dried rosemary
- ½ teaspoon dried basil
- ½ teaspoon dried thyme
- 2 small ripe tomatoes, puréed
- 120 g Parmesan cheese, grated

Directions:
1. Melt ½ tablespoon of butter in a sauté pan over medium-high heat. Now, cook the leek and garlic until tender and aromatic. Add the stock and wine to deglaze the pan.
2. Preheat the air fryer to 190°C.
3. Grease a casserole dish with the remaining ½ tablespoon of melted butter. Place the fish in the casserole dish. Add the seasonings. Top with the sautéed leek mixture. Add the tomato purée. Cook for 10 minutes in the preheated air fryer. Top with grated Parmesan cheese; cook an additional 7 minutes until the crumbs are golden. Bon appétit!

Salmon With Broccoli And Cheese

Servings: 2
Cooking Time: 18
Ingredients:
- 2 cups of broccoli
- ½ cup of butter, melted
- Salt and pepper, to taste
- Oil spray, for greasing
- 1 cup of grated cheddar cheese
- 1 pound of salmon, fillets

Directions:
1. Take a bowl and add broccoli to it.
2. Add salt and black pepper and spray it with oil.
3. Put the broccoli in the air fryer zone 1 backset.
4. Now rub the salmon fillets with salt, black pepper, and butter.
5. Put it into zone 2 baskets.
6. Set zone 1 to air fry mode for 5 minters at 400 degrees F.
7. Set zone 2 to air fry mode for 18 minutes at 390 degrees F.
8. Hit start to start the cooking.
9. Once done, serve and by placing it on serving plates.
10. Put the grated cheese on top of the salmon and serve.

Nutrition:
- (Per serving) Calories 966 | Fat 79.1 g| Sodium 808 mg | Carbs 6.8 g | Fiber 2.4g | Sugar 1.9g | Protein 61.2 g

Nutty Prawns With Amaretto Glaze

Servings: 10 To 12
Cooking Time: 10 Minutes
Ingredients:
- 120 g plain flour
- ½ teaspoon baking powder
- 1 teaspoon salt
- 2 eggs, beaten
- 120 ml milk
- 2 tablespoons olive or vegetable oil
- 185 g sliced almonds
- 900 g large prawns (about 32 to 40 prawns), peeled and deveined, tails left on
- 470 ml amaretto liqueur

Directions:
1. Combine the flour, baking powder and salt in a large bowl. Add the eggs, milk and oil and stir until it forms a smooth batter. Coarsely crush the sliced almonds into a second shallow dish with your hands.
2. Dry the prawns well with paper towels. Dip the prawns into the batter and shake off any excess batter, leaving just enough to lightly coat the prawns. Transfer the prawns to the dish with the almonds and coat completely. Place the coated prawns on a plate or baking sheet and when all the prawns have been coated, freeze the prawns for an 1 hour, or as long as a week before air frying.
3. Preheat the air fryer to 204°C.
4. Transfer frozen prawns to the two air fryer drawers. Air fry for 6 minutes. Turn the prawns over and air fry for an additional 4 minutes.
5. While the prawns are cooking, bring the Amaretto to a boil in a small saucepan on the stovetop. Lower the heat and simmer until it has reduced and thickened into a glaze, about 10 minutes.
6. Remove the prawns from the air fryer and brush both sides with the warm amaretto glaze. Serve warm.

Stuffed Mushrooms With Crab

Servings: 4
Cooking Time: 18 Minutes
Ingredients:
- 907g baby bella mushrooms
- cooking spray
- 2 teaspoons tony chachere's salt blend
- ¼ red onion, diced
- 2 celery ribs, diced
- 227g lump crab
- ½ cup seasoned bread crumbs
- 1 large egg
- ½ cup parmesan cheese, shredded
- 1 teaspoon oregano
- 1 teaspoon hot sauce

Directions:
1. Mix all the ingredients except the mushrooms in a bowl.
2. Divide the crab filling into the mushroom caps.
3. Place the caps in the air fryer baskets.
4. Return the air fryer basket 1 to Zone 1, and basket 2 to Zone 2 of the Ninja Foodi 2-Basket Air Fryer.
5. Choose the "Air Fry" mode for Zone 1 at 400 degrees F and 18 minutes of cooking time.
6. Select the "MATCH COOK" option to copy the settings for Zone 2.
7. Initiate cooking by pressing the START/PAUSE BUTTON.
8. Serve warm.

Nutrition:
- (Per serving) Calories 399 | Fat 16g | Sodium 537mg | Carbs 28g | Fiber 3g | Sugar 10g | Protein 35g

Marinated Salmon Fillets

Servings: 4
Cooking Time: 15 To 20 Minutes
Ingredients:
- 60 ml soy sauce
- 60 ml rice wine vinegar
- 1 tablespoon brown sugar
- 1 tablespoon olive oil
- 1 teaspoon mustard powder
- 1 teaspoon ground ginger
- ½ teaspoon freshly ground black pepper
- ½ teaspoon minced garlic
- 4 salmon fillets, 170 g each, skin-on
- Cooking spray

Directions:
1. In a small bowl, combine the soy sauce, rice wine vinegar, brown sugar, olive oil, mustard powder, ginger, black pepper, and garlic to make a marinade.
2. Place the fillets in a shallow baking dish and pour the marinade over them. Cover the baking dish and marinate for at least 1 hour in the refrigerator, turning the fillets occasionally to keep them coated in the marinade.
3. Preheat the air fryer to 190°C. Spray the two air fryer baskets lightly with cooking spray.
4. Shake off as much marinade as possible from the fillets and place them, skin-side down, in the two air fryer baskets in a single layer.
5. Air fry for 15 to 20 minutes for well done. The minimum internal temperature should be 65°C at the thickest part of the fillets.
6. Serve hot.

Fish Sandwich

Servings: 4
Cooking Time: 22 Minutes
Ingredients:
- 4 small cod fillets, skinless
- Salt and black pepper, to taste
- 2 tablespoons flour
- ¼ cup dried breadcrumbs
- Spray oil
- 9 ounces of frozen peas
- 1 tablespoon creme fraiche
- 12 capers
- 1 squeeze of lemon juice
- 4 bread rolls, cut in halve

Directions:
1. First, coat the cod fillets with flour, salt, and black pepper.
2. Then coat the fish with breadcrumbs.
3. Divide the coated codfish in the two crisper plates and spray them with cooking spray.
4. Return the crisper plate to the Ninja Foodi Dual Zone Air Fryer.
5. Choose the Air Fry mode for Zone 1 and set the temperature to 390 degrees F and the time to 17 minutes.
6. Select the "MATCH" button to copy the settings for Zone 2.
7. Initiate cooking by pressing the START/STOP button.
8. Meanwhile, boil peas in hot water for 5 minutes until soft.
9. Then drain the peas and transfer them to the blender.
10. Add capers, lemon juice, and crème fraiche to the blender.
11. Blend until it makes a smooth mixture.
12. Spread the peas crème mixture on top of 2 lower halves of the bread roll, and place the fish fillets on it.
13. Place the remaining bread slices on top.
14. Serve fresh.

Beef, Pork, And Lamb Recipes

Steak And Asparagus Bundles

Servings: 6
Cooking Time: 10 Minutes
Ingredients:
- 907g flank steak, cut into 6 pieces
- Salt and black pepper, to taste
- ½ cup tamari sauce
- 2 cloves garlic, crushed
- 455g asparagus, trimmed
- 3 capsicums, sliced
- ¼ cup balsamic vinegar
- 79 ml beef broth
- 2 tablespoons unsalted butter
- Olive oil spray

Directions:
1. Mix steaks with black pepper, tamari sauce, and garlic in a Ziplock bag.
2. Seal the bag, shake well and refrigerate for 1 hour.
3. Place the steaks on the working surface and top each with asparagus and capsicums.
4. Roll the steaks and secure them with toothpicks.
5. Place these rolls in the air fryer baskets.
6. Return the air fryer basket 1 to Zone 1, and basket 2 to Zone 2 of the Ninja Foodi 2-Basket Air Fryer.
7. Choose the "Air Fry" mode for Zone 1 and set the temperature to 400 degrees F and 10 minutes of cooking time.
8. Select the "MATCH COOK" option to copy the settings for Zone 2.
9. Initiate cooking by pressing the START/PAUSE BUTTON.
10. Meanwhile, cook broth with butter and vinegar in a saucepan.
11. Cook this mixture until reduced by half and adjust seasoning with black pepper and salt.
12. Serve the steak rolls with the prepared sauce.

Sausage And Cauliflower Arancini

Servings: 6
Cooking Time: 28 To 32 Minutes
Ingredients:
- Avocado oil spray
- 170 g Italian-seasoned sausage, casings removed
- 60 ml diced onion
- 1 teaspoon minced garlic
- 1 teaspoon dried thyme
- Sea salt and freshly ground black pepper, to taste
- 120 ml cauliflower rice
- 85 g cream cheese
- 110 g Cheddar cheese, shredded
- 1 large egg
- 120 ml finely ground blanched almond flour
- 60 ml finely grated Parmesan cheese
- Keto-friendly marinara sauce, for serving

Directions:
1. Spray a large skillet with oil and place it over medium-high heat. Once the skillet is hot, put the sausage in the skillet and cook for 7 minutes, breaking up the meat with the back of a spoon.
2. Reduce the heat to medium and add the onion. Cook for 5 minutes, then add the garlic, thyme, and salt and pepper to taste. Cook for 1 minute more.
3. Add the cauliflower rice and cream cheese to the skillet. Cook for 7 minutes, stirring frequently, until the cream cheese melts and the cauliflower is tender.
4. Remove the skillet from the heat and stir in the Cheddar cheese. Using a cookie scoop, form the mixture into 1½-inch balls. Place the balls on a parchment paper-lined baking sheet. Freeze for 30 minutes.
5. Place the egg in a shallow bowl and beat it with a fork. In a separate bowl, stir together the almond flour and Parmesan cheese.
6. Dip the cauliflower balls into the egg, then coat them with the almond flour mixture, gently pressing the mixture to the balls to adhere.
7. Set the air fryer to 204°C. Spray the cauliflower rice balls with oil, and arrange them in a single layer in the two air fryer drawers. Air fry for 5 minutes. Flip the rice balls and spray them with more oil. Air fry for 3 to 7 minutes longer, until the balls are golden brown.
8. Serve warm with marinara sauce.

Jerk-rubbed Pork Loin With Carrots And Sage

Servings: 4
Cooking Time: 35 Minutes
Ingredients:
- 1½ pounds pork loin
- 3 teaspoons canola oil, divided
- 2 tablespoons jerk seasoning
- 1-pound carrots, peeled, cut into 1-inch pieces
- 1 tablespoon honey
- ½ teaspoon kosher salt
- ½ teaspoon chopped fresh sage

Directions:
1. Place the pork loin in a pan or a dish with a high wall. Using a paper towel, pat the meat dry.
2. Rub 2 teaspoons of canola oil evenly over the pork with your hands. Then spread the jerk seasoning evenly over it with your hands.
3. Allow the pork loin to marinate for at least 10 minutes or up to 8 hours in the refrigerator after wrapping it in plastic wrap or sealing it in a plastic bag.
4. Toss the carrots with the remaining canola oil and ½ teaspoon of salt in a medium mixing bowl.
5. Place a crisper plate in each of the drawers. Put the marinated pork loin in the zone 1 drawer and place it in the unit. Place the carrots in the zone 2 drawer and place the drawer in the unit.
6. Select zone 1 and select AIR FRY. Set the temperature to 390 degrees F/ 200 degrees C and the time setting to 25 minutes. Select zone 2 and select AIR FRY. Set the temperature to 390 degrees F/ 200 degrees C and the time setting to 16 minutes. Select SYNC. Press START/STOP to begin cooking.
7. Check the pork loin for doneness after the zones have finished cooking. When the internal temperature of the loin hits 145°F on an instant-read thermometer, the pork is ready.
8. Allow the pork loin to rest for at least 5 minutes on a plate or cutting board.
9. Combine the carrots and sage in a mixing bowl.
10. When the pork loin has rested, slice it into the desired thickness of slices and serve with the carrots.

Nutrition:
- (Per serving) Calories 500 | Fat 19.8g | Sodium 680mg | Carbs 50.1g | Fiber 4.1g | Sugar 0g | Protein 27.9g

Sumptuous Pizza Tortilla Rolls

Servings: 4
Cooking Time: 6 Minutes
Ingredients:
- 1 teaspoon butter
- ½ medium onion, slivered
- ½ red or green pepper, julienned
- 110 g fresh white mushrooms, chopped
- 120 ml pizza sauce
- 8 flour tortillas
- 8 thin slices wafer-thin ham
- 24 pepperoni slices
- 235 ml shredded Mozzarella cheese
- Cooking spray

Directions:
1. Preheat the air fryer to 200°C.
2. Put butter, onions, pepper, and mushrooms in a baking pan. Bake in the preheated air fryer for 3 minutes. Stir and cook 3 to 4 minutes longer until just crisp and tender. Remove pan and set aside.
3. To assemble rolls, spread about 2 teaspoons of pizza sauce on one half of each tortilla. Top with a slice of ham and 3 slices of pepperoni. Divide sautéed vegetables among tortillas and top with cheese.
4. Roll up tortillas, secure with toothpicks if needed, and spray with oil.
5. Put the rolls in the two air fryer drawers and air fry for 4 minutes. Turn and air fry 4 minutes, until heated through and lightly browned.
6. Serve immediately.

Bbq Pork Chops

Servings: 4
Cooking Time: 12 Minutes
Ingredients:
- 4 pork chops
- Salt and black pepper to taste
- 1 package BBQ Shake & Bake
- Olive oil

Directions:
1. Season pork chops with black pepper, salt, BBQ shake and olive oil.
2. Place these chops in the air fryer baskets.
3. Return the air fryer basket 1 to Zone 1, and basket 2 to Zone 2 of the Ninja Foodi 2-Basket Air Fryer.
4. Choose the "Air Fry" mode for Zone 1 at 375 degrees F and 12 minutes of cooking time.
5. Select the "MATCH COOK" option to copy the settings for Zone 2.
6. Initiate cooking by pressing the START/PAUSE BUTTON.
7. Flip the pork chops once cooked halfway through.
8. Serve warm.

Meat And Rice Stuffed Peppers

Servings: 4
Cooking Time: 18 Minutes
Ingredients:
- 340 g lean beef mince
- 110 g lean pork mince
- 60 ml onion, minced
- 1 (425 g) can finely-chopped tomatoes
- 1 teaspoon Worcestershire sauce
- 1 teaspoon barbecue seasoning
- 1 teaspoon honey
- ½ teaspoon dried basil
- 120 ml cooked brown rice
- ½ teaspoon garlic powder
- ½ teaspoon oregano
- ½ teaspoon salt
- 2 small peppers, cut in half, stems removed, deseeded
- Cooking spray

Directions:
1. Preheat the zone 1 air fryer drawer to 182°C and spritz a baking pan with cooking spray.
2. Arrange the beef, pork, and onion in the baking pan and bake in the preheated air fryer drawer for 8 minutes. Break the ground meat into chunks halfway through the cooking.
3. Meanwhile, combine the tomatoes, Worcestershire sauce, barbecue seasoning, honey, and basil in a saucepan. Stir to mix well.
4. Transfer the cooked meat mixture to a large bowl and add the cooked rice, garlic powder, oregano, salt, and 60 ml of the tomato mixture. Stir to mix well.
5. Stuff the pepper halves with the mixture, then arrange the pepper halves in the zone 1 air fryer drawer and air fry for 10 minutes or until the peppers are lightly charred.
6. Serve the stuffed peppers with the remaining tomato sauce on top.

Cheeseburgers With Barbecue Potato Chips

Servings: 4
Cooking Time: 15 Minutes
Ingredients:
- FOR THE CHEESEBURGERS
- 1 pound ground beef (85 percent lean)
- ¼ teaspoon kosher salt
- ¼ teaspoon freshly ground black pepper
- ½ teaspoon olive oil
- 4 slices American cheese
- 4 hamburger rolls
- FOR THE POTATO CHIPS
- 2 large russet potatoes
- 2 teaspoons vegetable oil
- 1½ teaspoons smoked paprika
- 1 teaspoon light brown sugar
- ½ teaspoon garlic powder
- ½ teaspoon kosher salt
- ¼ teaspoon chili powder

Directions:
1. To prep the cheeseburgers: Season the beef with the salt and black pepper. Form the beef into 4 patties about 1 inch thick. Brush both sides of the beef patties with the oil.
2. To prep the potato chips: Fill a large bowl with ice water. Using a mandoline or sharp knife, cut the potatoes into very thin (⅛- to 1/16-inch) slices. Soak the potatoes in the ice water for 30 minutes.
3. Drain the potatoes and pat dry with a paper towel. Place in a large bowl and toss with the oil, smoked paprika, brown sugar, garlic powder, salt, and chili powder.
4. To cook the cheeseburgers and potato chips: Install a crisper plate in each of the two baskets. Place the burgers in the Zone 1 basket and insert the basket in the unit. Place the potato slices in the Zone 2 basket and insert the basket in the unit.
5. Select Zone 1, select AIR FRY, set the temperature to 390°F, and set the time to 12 minutes.
6. Select Zone 2, select AIR FRY, set the temperature to 390°F, and set the time to 15 minutes. Select SMART FINISH.
7. Press START/PAUSE to begin cooking.
8. At 5-minute intervals, press START/PAUSE. Remove the Zone 2 basket and shake the potato chips to keep them from sticking to each other. Reinsert the basket and press START/PAUSE to resume cooking.
9. When cooking is complete, the burgers should be cooked to your preferred doneness and the potato chips should be crisp and golden brown.
10. Top each burger patty in the basket with a slice of cheese. Turn the air fryer off and let the cheese melt inside the unit, or cover the basket with aluminum foil and let stand for 1 to 2 minutes, until the cheese is melted. Serve the cheeseburgers on buns with the chips on the side.

Nutrition:
- (Per serving) Calories: 475; Total fat: 22g; Saturated fat: 8g; Carbohydrates: 38g; Fiber: 2g; Protein: 32g; Sodium: 733mg

Garlic Butter Steaks

Servings: 2
Cooking Time: 25 Minutes
Ingredients:
- 2 (6 ounces each) sirloin steaks or ribeyes
- 2 tablespoons unsalted butter
- 1 clove garlic, crushed
- ½ teaspoon dried parsley
- ½ teaspoon dried rosemary
- Salt and pepper, to taste

Directions:
1. Season the steaks with salt and pepper and set them to rest for about 2 hours before cooking.
2. Put the butter in a bowl. Add the garlic, parsley, and rosemary. Allow the butter to soften.
3. Whip together with a fork or spoon once the butter has softened.
4. When you're ready to cook, install a crisper plate in both drawers. Place the sirloin steaks in a single layer in each drawer. Insert the drawers into the unit.
5. Select zone 1, select AIR FRY, set temperature to 360 degrees F/ 180 degrees C, and set time to 10 minutes. Select MATCH to match zone 2 settings to zone 1. Select START/STOP to begin.
6. Once done, serve with the garlic butter.

Nutrition:
- (Per serving) Calories 519 | Fat 36g | Sodium 245mg | Carbs 1g | Fiber 0g | Sugar 0g | Protein 46g

Pork Chops With Apples

Servings: 2
Cooking Time: 20 Minutes
Ingredients:
- ½ small red cabbage, sliced
- 1 apple, sliced
- 1 sweet onion, sliced
- 2 tablespoons oil
- ½ teaspoon cumin
- ½ teaspoon paprika
- Salt and black pepper, to taste
- 2 boneless pork chops (1" thick)

Directions:
1. Toss pork chops with apple and the rest of the ingredients in a bowl.
2. Divide the mixture in the air fryer baskets.
3. Return the air fryer basket 1 to Zone 1, and basket 2 to Zone 2 of the Ninja Foodi 2-Basket Air Fryer.
4. Choose the "Air Fry" mode for Zone 1 and set the temperature to 400 degrees F and 15 minutes of cooking time.
5. Select the "MATCH COOK" option to copy the settings for Zone 2.
6. Initiate cooking by pressing the START/PAUSE BUTTON.
7. Serve warm.

Glazed Steak Recipe

Servings: 2
Cooking Time: 25
Ingredients:
- 1 pound of beef steaks
- ½ cup, soy sauce
- Salt and black pepper, to taste
- 1 tablespoon of vegetable oil
- 1 teaspoon of grated ginger
- 4 cloves garlic, minced
- 1/4 cup brown sugar

Directions:
1. Take a bowl and whisk together soy sauce, salt, pepper, vegetable oil, garlic, brown sugar, and ginger.
2. Once a paste is made rub the steak with the marinate
3. Let it sit for 30 minutes.
4. After 30 minutes add the steak to the air fryer basket and set it to AIR BROIL mode at 400 degrees F for 18-22 minutes.
5. After 10 minutes, hit pause and takeout the basket.
6. Let the steak flip and again let it AIR BROIL for the remaining minutes.
7. Once 25 minutes of cooking cycle completes.
8. Take out the steak and let it rest. Serve by cutting into slices.
9. Enjoy.

Nutrition:
- (Per serving) Calories 563| Fat 21 g| Sodium 156mg | Carbs 20.6g | Fiber 0.3 g| Sugar 17.8 g | Protein 69.4 g

Five-spice Pork Belly

Servings: 4
Cooking Time: 17 Minutes
Ingredients:
- 450 g unsalted pork belly
- 2 teaspoons Chinese five-spice powder
- Sauce:
- 1 tablespoon coconut oil
- 1 (1-inch) piece fresh ginger, peeled and grated
- 2 cloves garlic, minced
- 120 ml beef or chicken stock
- ¼ to 120 ml liquid or powdered sweetener
- 3 tablespoons wheat-free tamari
- 1 spring onion, sliced, plus more for garnish

Directions:
1. Spray the two air fryer drawers with avocado oil. Preheat the air fryer to 204°C. 2. Cut the pork belly into ½-inch-thick slices and season well on all sides with the five-spice powder. Place the slices in a single layer in the two air fryer drawers and cook for 8 minutes, or until cooked to your liking, flipping halfway through. 3. While the pork belly cooks, make the sauce: Heat the coconut oil in a small saucepan over medium heat. Add the ginger and garlic and sauté for 1 minute, or until fragrant. Add the stock, sweetener, and tamari and simmer for 10 to 15 minutes, until thickened. Add the spring onion and cook for another minute, until the spring onion is softened. Taste and adjust the seasoning to your liking. 4. Transfer the pork belly to a large bowl. Pour the sauce over the pork belly and coat well. Place the pork belly slices on a serving platter and garnish with sliced spring onions. 5. Best served fresh. Store leftovers in an airtight container in the fridge for up to 4 days. Reheat in a preheated 204°C air fryer for 3 minutes, or until heated through.

Roast Beef With Yorkshire Pudding

Servings: 6
Cooking Time: 40 Minutes
Ingredients:
- FOR THE ROAST BEEF
- 3-pound beef roast, trimmed
- 1 tablespoon vegetable oil
- ½ teaspoon kosher salt
- ½ teaspoon freshly ground black pepper
- ½ teaspoon garlic powder
- ½ teaspoon onion powder
- ½ teaspoon dried thyme
- FOR THE YORKSHIRE PUDDING
- 3 large eggs
- ¾ cup whole milk
- 2 tablespoons beef broth
- ¾ cup all-purpose flour
- ½ teaspoon kosher salt
- 2 teaspoons unsalted butter

Directions:
1. To prep the roast beef: If necessary, trim the beef roast to fit in the Zone 1 basket. Rub the beef with the oil.
2. In a small bowl, combine the salt, black pepper, garlic powder, onion powder, and thyme. Rub the spice mixture all over the beef roast.
3. To prep the Yorkshire pudding: In a large bowl, whisk the eggs, milk, and beef broth until well combined. Whisk in the flour and salt to form a thin batter.
4. To cook the beef and Yorkshire pudding: Install a crisper plate in the Zone 1 basket. Place the beef roast in the basket and insert the basket in the unit. Place the butter in the Zone 2 basket and insert the basket in the unit.
5. Select Zone 1, select AIR FRY, set the temperature to 375°F, and set the time to 40 minutes for a medium-rare roast (set to 50 minutes for medium or 60 minutes for well done).
6. Select Zone 2, select BAKE, set the temperature to 400°F, and set the time to 20 minutes. Select SMART FINISH.
7. Press START/PAUSE to begin cooking.
8. When the Zone 2 timer reads 18 minutes, press START/PAUSE. Remove the basket and pour the batter into it. Reinsert the basket and press START/PAUSE to resume cooking.
9. When cooking is complete, the beef should be cooked to your liking and the Yorkshire pudding should be fluffy on the edges and set in the center.
10. Remove the beef from the basket and let rest for at least 15 minutes before slicing.
11. Cut the Yorkshire pudding into 6 servings and serve the sliced beef on top.

Nutrition:
- (Per serving) Calories: 517; Total fat: 26g; Saturated fat: 9.5g; Carbohydrates: 13g; Fiber: 0.5g; Protein: 52g; Sodium: 354mg

New York Strip Steak

Servings: 2
Cooking Time: 10 Minutes
Ingredients:
- 1 (4½-ounce) New York strip steaks
- 1½ teaspoons olive oil
- Salt and ground black pepper, as required

Directions:
1. Grease each basket of "Zone 1" and "Zone 2" of Ninja Foodi 2-Basket Air Fryer.
2. Press "Zone 1" and "Zone 2" and then rotate the knob for each zone to select "Air Fry".
3. Set the temperature to 400 degrees F/ 200 degrees C for both zones and then set the time for 5 minutes to preheat.
4. Coat the steaks with oil and then sprinkle with salt and black pepper evenly.
5. After preheating, arrange the steak into the basket of each zone.
6. Slide each basket into Air Fryer and set the time for 10 minutes.
7. While cooking, flip the steak once halfway through.
8. After cooking time is completed, remove the steaks from Air Fryer and place onto a platter for about 10 minutes.
9. Cut each steak into desired size slices and serve immediately.

Kielbasa Sausage With Pineapple And Kheema Meatloaf

Servings: 6 To 8
Cooking Time: 15 Minutes
Ingredients:
- Kielbasa Sausage with Pineapple:
- 340 g kielbasa sausage, cut into ½-inch slices
- 1 (230 g) can pineapple chunks in juice, drained
- 235 ml pepper chunks
- 1 tablespoon barbecue seasoning
- 1 tablespoon soy sauce
- Cooking spray
- Kheema Meatloaf:
- 450 g 85% lean beef mince
- 2 large eggs, lightly beaten
- 235 ml diced brown onion
- 60 ml chopped fresh coriander
- 1 tablespoon minced fresh ginger
- 1 tablespoon minced garlic
- 2 teaspoons garam masala
- 1 teaspoon coarse or flaky salt
- 1 teaspoon ground turmeric
- 1 teaspoon cayenne pepper
- ½ teaspoon ground cinnamon
- ⅛ teaspoon ground cardamom

Directions:
1. Make the Kielbasa Sausage with Pineapple :
2. Preheat the air fryer to 200°C. Spritz the zone 1 air fryer drawer with cooking spray.
3. Combine all the ingredients in a large bowl. Toss to mix well.
4. Pour the sausage mixture in the preheated zone 1 air fryer drawer.
5. Air fry for 10 minutes or until the sausage is lightly browned and the pepper and pineapple are soft. Shake the drawer halfway through. Serve immediately.
6. Make the Kheema Meatloaf :
7. In a large bowl, gently mix the beef mince, eggs, onion, coriander, ginger, garlic, garam masala, salt, turmeric, cayenne, cinnamon, and cardamom until thoroughly combined.
8. Place the seasoned meat in a baking pan. Place the pan in the zone 2 air fryer drawer. Set the temperature to 176°C for 15 minutes. Use a meat thermometer to ensure the meat loaf has reached an internal temperature of 72°C .
9. Drain the fat and liquid from the pan and let stand for 5 minutes before slicing.
10. Slice and serve hot.

Asian Pork Skewers

Servings: 4
Cooking Time: 30 Minutes
Ingredients:
- 450g pork shoulder, sliced
- 30g ginger, peeled and crushed
- ½ tablespoon crushed garlic
- 67½ml soy sauce
- 22½ml honey
- 22½ml rice vinegar
- 10ml toasted sesame oil
- 8 skewers

Directions:
1. Pound the pork slices with a mallet.
2. Mix ginger, garlic, soy sauce, honey, rice vinegar, and sesame oil in a bowl.
3. Add pork slices to the marinade and mix well to coat.
4. Cover and marinate the pork for 30 minutes.
5. Thread the pork on the wooden skewers and place them in the air fryer baskets.
6. Return the air fryer basket 1 to Zone 1, and basket 2 to Zone 2 of the Ninja Foodi 2-Basket Air Fryer.
7. Choose the "Air Fry" mode for Zone 1 and set the temperature to 350 degrees F and 25 minutes of cooking time.
8. Select the "MATCH COOK" option to copy the settings for Zone 2.
9. Initiate cooking by pressing the START/PAUSE BUTTON.
10. Flip the skewers once cooked halfway through.
11. Serve warm.

Steak In Air Fry

Servings:1
Cooking Time:20
Ingredients:
- 2 teaspoons of canola oil
- 1 tablespoon of Montreal steaks seasoning
- 1 pound of beef steak

Directions:
1. The first step is to season the steak on both sides with canola oil and then rub a generous amount of steak seasoning all over.
2. We are using the AIR BROIL feature of the ninja air fryer and it works with one basket.
3. Put the steak in the basket and set it to AIR BROIL at 450 degrees F for 20 -22 minutes.
4. After 7 minutes, hit pause and take out the basket to flip the steak, and cover it with foil on top, for the remaining 14 minutes.
5. Once done, serve the medium-rare steak and enjoy it by resting for 10 minutes.
6. Serve by cutting in slices.
7. Enjoy.

Nutrition:
- (Per serving) Calories 935| Fat 37.2g| Sodium 1419mg | Carbs 0g | Fiber 0g| Sugar 0g | Protein137.5 g

Turkey And Beef Meatballs

Servings: 6
Cooking Time: 24 Minutes.
Ingredients:
- 1 medium shallot, minced
- 2 tablespoons olive oil
- 3 garlic cloves, minced
- ¼ cup panko crumbs
- 2 tablespoons whole milk
- ⅔ lb. lean ground beef
- ⅓ lb. bulk turkey sausage
- 1 large egg, lightly beaten
- ¼ cup parsley, chopped
- 1 tablespoon fresh thyme, chopped
- 1 tablespoon fresh rosemary, chopped
- 1 tablespoon Dijon mustard
- ½ teaspoon salt

Directions:
1. Preheat your oven to 400 degrees F. Place a medium non-stick pan over medium-high heat.
2. Add oil and shallot, then sauté for 2 minutes.
3. Toss in the garlic and cook for 1 minute.
4. Remove this pan from the heat.
5. Whisk panko with milk in a large bowl and leave it for 5 minutes.
6. Add cooked shallot mixture and mix well.
7. Stir in egg, parsley, turkey sausage, beef, thyme, rosemary, salt, and mustard.
8. Mix well, then divide the mixture into 1 ½-inch balls.
9. Divide these balls into the two crisper plates and spray them with cooking oil.
10. Return the crisper plates to the Ninja Foodi Dual Zone Air Fryer.
11. Choose the Air Fry mode for Zone 1 and set the temperature to 400 degrees F and the time to 21 minutes.
12. Select the "MATCH" button to copy the settings for Zone 2.
13. Initiate cooking by pressing the START/STOP button.
14. Serve warm.

Nutrition:
- (Per serving) Calories 551 | Fat 31g |Sodium 1329mg | Carbs 1.5g | Fiber 0.8g | Sugar 0.4g | Protein 64g

Easy Breaded Pork Chops

Servings: 8
Cooking Time: 20 Minutes
Ingredients:
- 1 egg
- 118ml milk
- 8 pork chops
- 1 packet ranch seasoning
- 238g breadcrumbs
- Pepper
- Salt

Directions:
1. In a small bowl, whisk the egg and milk.
2. In a separate shallow dish, mix breadcrumbs, ranch seasoning, pepper, and salt.
3. Dip each pork chop in the egg mixture, then coat with breadcrumbs.
4. Insert a crisper plate in the Ninja Foodi air fryer baskets.
5. Place the coated pork chops in both baskets.
6. Select zone 1, then select air fry mode and set the temperature to 360 degrees F for 12 minutes. Press "match" to match zone 2 settings to zone 1. Press "start/stop" to begin. Turn halfway through.

Mongolian Beef With Sweet Chili Brussels Sprouts

Servings: 4
Cooking Time: 20 Minutes
Ingredients:
- FOR THE MONGOLIAN BEEF
- 1 pound flank steak, cut into thin strips
- 1 tablespoon olive oil
- 2 tablespoons cornstarch
- ½ cup reduced-sodium soy sauce
- ½ cup packed light brown sugar
- 1 tablespoon chili paste (optional)
- 1 tablespoon minced garlic
- 1 tablespoon minced fresh ginger
- 2 scallions, chopped
- FOR THE BRUSSELS SPROUTS
- 1 pound Brussels sprouts, halved lengthwise
- 1 tablespoon olive oil
- ½ cup gochujang sauce
- 2 tablespoons rice vinegar
- 1 tablespoon reduced-sodium soy sauce
- 1 tablespoon light brown sugar
- 1 teaspoon fresh garlic

Directions:
1. To prep the Mongolian beef: In a large bowl, combine the flank steak and olive oil and toss to coat. Add the cornstarch and toss to coat.
2. In a small bowl, whisk together the soy sauce, brown sugar, chili paste (if using), garlic, and ginger. Set the soy sauce mixture aside.
3. To prep the Brussels sprouts: In a large bowl, combine the Brussels sprouts and oil and toss to coat.
4. In a small bowl, whisk together the gochujang sauce, vinegar, soy sauce, brown sugar, and garlic. Set the chili sauce mixture aside.
5. To cook the beef and Brussels sprouts: Install a crisper plate in each of the two baskets. Place the beef in the Zone 1 basket and insert the basket in the unit. Place the Brussels sprouts in the Zone 2 basket and insert the basket in the unit.
6. Select Zone 1, select AIR FRY, set the temperature to 390°F, and set the time to 15 minutes.
7. Select Zone 2, select AIR FRY, set the temperature to 400°F, and set the time to 20 minutes. Select SMART FINISH.
8. Press START/PAUSE to begin cooking.
9. When both timers read 5 minutes, press START/PAUSE. Remove the Zone 1 basket, add the reserved soy sauce mixture and the scallions, and toss with the beef. Reinsert the basket. Remove the Zone 2 basket, add the reserved chili sauce mixture, and toss with the Brussels sprouts. Reinsert the basket and press START/PAUSE to resume cooking.
10. When cooking is complete, the steak should be cooked through and the Brussels sprouts tender and slightly caramelized. Serve warm.

Nutrition:
- (Per serving) Calories: 481; Total fat: 16g; Saturated fat: 4.5g; Carbohydrates: 60g; Fiber: 5g; Protein: 27g; Sodium: 2,044mg

Garlic Butter Steak Bites

Servings: 3
Cooking Time: 16 Minutes
Ingredients:
- Oil, for spraying
- 450 g boneless steak, cut into 1-inch pieces
- 2 tablespoons olive oil
- 1 teaspoon Worcestershire sauce
- ½ teaspoon granulated garlic
- ½ teaspoon salt
- ¼ teaspoon freshly ground black pepper

Directions:
1. Preheat the air fryer to 204°C. Line the two air fryer drawers with parchment and spray lightly with oil.
2. In a medium bowl, combine the steak, olive oil, Worcestershire sauce, garlic, salt, and black pepper and toss until evenly coated.
3. Place the steak in a single layer in the two prepared drawers.
4. Cook for 10 to 16 minutes, flipping every 3 to 4 minutes. The total cooking time will depend on the thickness of the meat and your preferred doneness. If you want it well done, it may take up to 5 additional minutes.

Spicy Lamb Chops

Servings: 4
Cooking Time: 15
Ingredients:
- 12 lamb chops, bone-in
- Salt and black pepper, to taste
- ½ teaspoon of lemon zest
- 1 tablespoon of lemon juice
- 1 teaspoon of paprika
- 1 teaspoon of garlic powder
- ½ teaspoon of Italian seasoning
- ¼ teaspoon of onion powder

Directions:
1. Add the lamb chops to the bowl and sprinkle salt, garlic powder, Italian seasoning, onion powder, black pepper, lemon zest, lemon juice, and paprika.
2. Rub the chops well, and divide it between both the baskets of the air fryer.
3. Set zone 1 basket to 400 degrees F, for 15 minutes at AIR FRY mode.
4. Select MATCH for zone2 basket.
5. After 10 minutes, take out the baskets and flip the chops cook for the remaining minutes, and then serve.

Nutrition:
- (Per serving) Calories 787| Fat 45.3g| Sodium1 mg | Carbs 16.1g | Fiber0.3g | Sugar 0.4g | Protein 75.3g

Barbecue Ribs With Roasted Green Beans And Shallots

Servings: 4
Cooking Time: 40 Minutes
Ingredients:
- FOR THE RIBS
- 1 tablespoon light brown sugar
- 1 tablespoon smoked paprika
- 1 tablespoon chili powder
- 2 teaspoons kosher salt
- 1 teaspoon freshly ground black pepper
- 1 teaspoon garlic powder
- ¼ teaspoon cayenne pepper (optional)
- 2 pounds pork ribs
- 1 cup barbecue sauce (your favorite), for serving
- FOR THE GREEN BEANS AND SHALLOTS
- 1 pound green beans, trimmed
- 2 shallots, sliced
- 1 tablespoon olive oil
- ¼ teaspoon kosher salt

Directions:
1. To prep the ribs: In a small bowl, combine the brown sugar, paprika, chili powder, salt, black pepper, garlic powder, and cayenne (if using).
2. Rub the spice blend all over both sides of the ribs.
3. To prep the green beans and shallots: In a large bowl, combine the green beans, shallots, and oil. Toss to coat. Season with the salt.
4. To cook the ribs and vegetables: Install a crisper plate in each of the two baskets. Place the ribs in the Zone 1 basket and insert the basket in the unit. Place the green beans in the Zone 2 basket and insert the basket in the unit.
5. Select Zone 1, select AIR FRY, set the temperature to 375°F, and set the time to 40 minutes.
6. Select Zone 2, select ROAST, set the temperature to 400°F, and set the time to 20 minutes. Select SMART FINISH.
7. Press START/PAUSE to begin cooking.
8. When the Zone 1 timer reads 10 minutes, press START/PAUSE. Increase the temperature of Zone 1 to 400°F. Press START/PAUSE to resume cooking.
9. When cooking is complete, an instant-read thermometer inserted into the ribs should read 170°F and the green beans should be tender-crisp. Serve topped with your favorite barbecue sauce.

Nutrition:
- (Per serving) Calories: 541; Total fat: 27g; Saturated fat: 9g; Carbohydrates: 48g; Fiber: 4.5g; Protein: 28g; Sodium: 1,291mg

Meatballs

Servings: 4
Cooking Time: 20 Minutes
Ingredients:
- 450g ground beef
- 59ml milk
- 45g parmesan cheese, grated
- 50g breadcrumbs
- ½ tsp Italian seasoning
- 2 garlic cloves, minced
- Pepper
- Salt

Directions:
1. In a bowl, mix the meat and remaining ingredients until well combined.
2. Insert a crisper plate in the Ninja Foodi air fryer baskets.
3. Make small balls from the meat mixture and place them in both baskets.
4. Select zone 1, then select "air fry" mode and set the temperature to 375 degrees F for 15 minutes. Press "match" and "start/stop" to begin.

Ham Burger Patties

Servings: 2
Cooking Time: 17
Ingredients:
- 1 pound of ground beef
- Salt and pepper, to taste
- ½ teaspoon of red chili powder
- ¼ teaspoon of coriander powder
- 2 tablespoons of chopped onion
- 1 green chili, chopped
- Oil spray for greasing
- 2 large potato wedges

Directions:
1. Oil greases the air fryer baskets with oil spray.
2. Add potato wedges in the zone 1 basket.
3. Take a bowl and add minced beef in it and add salt, pepper, chili powder, coriander powder, green chili, and chopped onion.
4. mix well and make two burger patties with wet hands place the two patties in the air fryer zone 2 basket.
5. put the basket inside the air fryer.
6. now, set time for zone 1 for 12 minutes using AIR FRY mode at 400 degrees F.
7. Select the MATCH button for zone 2.
8. once the time of cooking complete, take out the baskets.
9. flip the patties and shake the potatoes wedges.
10. again, set time of zone 1 basket for 4 minutes at 400 degrees F
11. Select the MATCH button for the second basket.
12. Once it's done, serve and enjoy.

Nutrition:
- (Per serving) Calories875 | Fat21.5g | Sodium 622mg | Carbs 88g | Fiber10.9 g| Sugar 3.4g | Protein 78.8g

Taco Seasoned Steak

Servings: 6
Cooking Time: 30 Minutes
Ingredients:
- 1 (1-pound) flank steaks
- 1½ tablespoons taco seasoning rub

Directions:
1. Grease each basket of "Zone 1" and "Zone 2" of Ninja Foodi 2-Basket Air Fryer.
2. Press "Zone 1" and "Zone 2" and then rotate the knob for each zone to select "Bake".
3. Set the temperature to 420 degrees F/ 215 degrees C for both zones and then set the time for 5 minutes to preheat.
4. Rub the steaks with taco seasoning evenly.
5. After preheating, arrange the steak into the basket of each zone.
6. Slide each basket into Air Fryer and set the time for 30 minutes.
7. After cooking time is completed, remove the steaks from Air Fryer and place onto a cutting board for about 10-15 minutes before slicing.
8. With a sharp knife, cut each steak into desired size slices and serve.

Sweet And Spicy Country-style Ribs

Servings: 4
Cooking Time: 25 Minutes
Ingredients:
- 2 tablespoons brown sugar
- 2 tablespoons smoked paprika
- 1 teaspoon garlic powder
- 1 teaspoon onion granules
- 1 teaspoon mustard powder
- 1 teaspoon ground cumin
- 1 teaspoon coarse or flaky salt
- 1 teaspoon black pepper
- ¼ to ½ teaspoon cayenne pepper
- 680 g boneless pork steaks
- 235 ml barbecue sauce

Directions:
1. In a small bowl, stir together the brown sugar, paprika, garlic powder, onion granules, mustard powder, cumin, salt, black pepper, and cayenne. Mix until well combined.
2. Pat the ribs dry with a paper towel. Generously sprinkle the rub evenly over both sides of the ribs and rub in with your fingers.
3. Place the ribs in the two air fryer drawers. Set the air fryer to 176°C for 15 minutes. Turn the ribs and brush with 120 ml of the barbecue sauce. Cook for an additional 10 minutes. Use a meat thermometer to ensure the pork has reached an internal temperature of 64°C.
4. Serve with remaining barbecue sauce.

Bacon Wrapped Pork Tenderloin

Servings: 2
Cooking Time: 20 Minutes
Ingredients:
- ½ teaspoon salt
- ¼ teaspoon black pepper
- 1 pork tenderloin
- 6 center cut strips bacon
- cooking string

Directions:
1. Cut two bacon strips in half and place them on the working surface.
2. Place the other bacon strips on top and lay the tenderloin over the bacon strip.
3. Wrap the bacon around the tenderloin and tie the roast with a kitchen string.
4. Place the roast in the first air fryer basket.
5. Return the air fryer basket 1 to Zone 1, and basket 2 to Zone 2 of the Ninja Foodi 2-Basket Air Fryer.
6. Choose the "Air Fry" mode for Zone 1 and set the temperature to 400 degrees F and 20 minutes of cooking time.
7. Initiate cooking by pressing the START/PAUSE BUTTON.
8. Slice and serve warm.

Roasted Beef

Servings: 8
Cooking Time: 50 Minutes
Ingredients:
- 1 (1-pound) beef roast
- Salt and ground black pepper, as required

Directions:
1. Grease each basket of "Zone 1" and "Zone 2" of Ninja Foodi 2-Basket Air Fryer.
2. Press "Zone 1" and "Zone 2" and then rotate the knob for each zone to select "Roast".
3. Set the temperature to 350 degrees F/ 175 degrees C for both zones and then set the time for 5 minutes to preheat.
4. Rub ach roast with salt and black pepper generously.
5. After preheating, arrange the roast into the basket of each zone.
6. Slide each basket into Air Fryer and set the time for 50 minutes.
7. After cooking time is completed, remove each roast from Air Fryer and place onto a platter for about 10 minutes before slicing.
8. With a sharp knife, cut each roast into desired-sized slices and serve.

Meatloaf

Servings: 6
Cooking Time: 25 Minutes
Ingredients:
- For the meatloaf:
- 2 pounds ground beef
- 2 eggs, beaten
- 2 cups old-fashioned oats, regular or gluten-free
- ½ cup evaporated milk
- ½ cup chopped onion
- ½ teaspoon garlic salt
- For the sauce:
- 1 cup ketchup
- ¾ cup brown sugar, packed
- ¼ cup chopped onion
- ½ teaspoon liquid smoke
- ¼ teaspoon garlic powder
- Olive oil cooking spray

Directions:
1. In a large bowl, combine all the meatloaf ingredients.
2. Spray 2 sheets of foil with olive oil cooking spray.
3. Form the meatloaf mixture into a loaf shape, cut in half, and place each half on one piece of foil.
4. Roll the foil up a bit on the sides. Allow it to be slightly open.
5. Put all the sauce ingredients in a saucepan and whisk until combined on medium-low heat. This should only take 1–2 minutes
6. Install a crisper plate in both drawers. Place half the meatloaf in the zone 1 drawer and half in zone 2's, then insert the drawers into the unit.
7. Select zone 1, select AIR FRY, set temperature to 390 degrees F/ 200 degrees C, and set time to 25 minutes. Select MATCH to match zone 2 settings to zone 1. Press the START/STOP button to begin cooking.
8. When the time reaches 20 minutes, press START/STOP to pause the unit. Remove the drawers and coat the meatloaf with the sauce using a brush. Re-insert the drawers into the unit and press START/STOP to resume cooking.
9. Carefully remove and serve.

Nutrition:
- (Per serving) Calories 727 | Fat 34g | Sodium 688mg | Carbs 57g | Fiber 3g | Sugar 34g | Protein 49g

Rosemary And Garlic Lamb Chops

Servings: 4
Cooking Time: 15 Minutes
Ingredients:
- 8 lamb chops
- 3 tablespoons olive oil
- 2 tablespoons chopped fresh rosemary
- 1 teaspoon garlic powder or 3 cloves garlic, minced
- 1 teaspoon salt, or to taste
- ½ teaspoon black pepper, or to taste

Directions:
1. Dry the lamb chops with a paper towel.
2. Combine the olive oil, rosemary, garlic, salt, and pepper in a large mixing bowl. Toss the lamb in the marinade gently to coat it. Cover and set aside to marinate for 1 hour or up to overnight.
3. Install a crisper plate in both drawers. Place half the lamb chops in the zone 1 drawer and half in zone 2's, then insert the drawers into the unit.
4. Select zone 1, select AIR FRY, set temperature to 390 degrees F/ 200 degrees C, and set time to 15 minutes. Select MATCH to match zone 2 settings to zone 1. Press the START/STOP button to begin cooking.
5. When the time reaches 10 minutes, press START/STOP to pause the unit. Remove the drawers and flip the chops. Re-insert the drawers into the unit and press START/STOP to resume cooking.
6. Serve and enjoy!

Nutrition:
- (Per serving) Calories 427 | Fat 34g | Sodium 668mg | Carbs 1g | Fiber 1g | Sugar 1g | Protein 31g

Rosemary Ribeye Steaks And Mongolian-style Beef

Servings: 6
Cooking Time: 15 Minutes
Ingredients:
- Rosemary Ribeye Steaks:
- 60 ml butter
- 1 clove garlic, minced
- Salt and ground black pepper, to taste
- 1½ tablespoons balsamic vinegar
- 60 ml rosemary, chopped
- 2 ribeye steaks
- Mongolian-Style Beef:
- Oil, for spraying
- 60 ml cornflour
- 450 g bavette or skirt steak, thinly sliced
- 180 ml packed light brown sugar
- 120 ml soy sauce
- 2 teaspoons toasted sesame oil
- 1 tablespoon minced garlic
- ½ teaspoon ground ginger
- 120 ml water
- Cooked white rice or ramen noodles, for serving

Directions:
1. Make the Rosemary Ribeye Steaks :
2. Melt the butter in a skillet over medium heat. Add the garlic and fry until fragrant.
3. Remove the skillet from the heat and add the salt, pepper, and vinegar. Allow it to cool.
4. Add the rosemary, then pour the mixture into a Ziploc bag.
5. Put the ribeye steaks in the bag and shake well, coating the meat well. Refrigerate for an hour, then allow to sit for a further twenty minutes.
6. Preheat the zone 1 air fryer drawer to 204°C.
7. Air fry the ribeye steaks for 15 minutes.
8. Take care when removing the steaks from the air fryer and plate up.
9. Serve immediately.
10. Make the Mongolian-Style Beef :
11. Line the zone 2 air fryer drawer with parchment and spray lightly with oil.
12. Place the cornflour in a bowl and dredge the steak until evenly coated. Shake off any excess cornflour.
13. Place the steak in the prepared drawer and spray lightly with oil.
14. Roast at 200°C for 5 minutes, flip, and cook for another 5 minutes.
15. In a small saucepan, combine the brown sugar, soy sauce, sesame oil, garlic, ginger, and water and bring to a boil over medium-high heat, stirring frequently. Remove from the heat.
16. Transfer the meat to the sauce and toss until evenly coated. Let sit for about 5 minutes so the steak absorbs the flavors. Serve with white rice or ramen noodles.

Chinese Bbq Pork

Servings: 35
Cooking Time: 25
Ingredients:
- 4 tablespoons of soy sauce
- ¼ cup red wine
- 2 tablespoons of oyster sauce
- ¼ tablespoons of hoisin sauce
- ¼ cup honey
- ¼ cup brown sugar
- Pinch of salt
- Pinch of black pepper
- 1 teaspoon of ginger garlic, paste
- 1 teaspoon of five-spice powder
- 1.5 pounds of pork shoulder, sliced

Directions:
1. Take a bowl and mix all the ingredients listed under sauce ingredients.
2. Transfer half of it to a sauce pan and let it cook for 10 minutes.
3. Set it aside.
4. Let the pork marinate in the remaining sauce for 2 hours.
5. Afterward, put the pork slices in the basket and set it to AIRBORIL mode 450 degrees for 25 minutes.
6. Make sure the internal temperature is above 160 degrees F once cooked.
7. If not add a few more minutes to the overall cooking time.
8. Once done, take it out and baste it with prepared sauce.
9. Serve and Enjoy.

Nutrition:
- (Per serving) Calories 1239| Fat 73 g| Sodium 2185 mg | Carbs 57.3 g | Fiber 0.4g| Sugar 53.7 g | Protein 81.5 g

Gochujang Brisket

Servings: 6
Cooking Time: 55 Minutes.
Ingredients:
- ½ tablespoons sweet paprika
- ½ teaspoon toasted sesame oil
- 2 lbs. beef brisket, cut into 4 pieces
- Salt, to taste
- ⅛ cup Gochujang, Korean chili paste
- Black pepper, to taste
- 1 small onion, diced
- 2 garlic cloves, minced
- 1 teaspoon Asian fish sauce
- 1 ½ tablespoons peanut oil, as needed
- ½ tablespoon fresh ginger, grated
- ¼ teaspoon red chili flakes
- ½ cup of water
- 1 tablespoon ketchup
- 1 tablespoon soy sauce

Directions:
1. Thoroughly rub the beef brisket with olive oil, paprika, chili flakes, black pepper, and salt.
2. Cut the brisket in half, then divide the beef in the two crisper plate.
3. Return the crisper plate to the Ninja Foodi Dual Zone Air Fryer.
4. Choose the Air Fry mode for Zone 1 and set the temperature to 390 degrees F and the time to 35 minutes.
5. Select the "MATCH" button to copy the settings for Zone 2.
6. Initiate cooking by pressing the START/STOP button.
7. Flip the brisket halfway through, and resume cooking.
8. Meanwhile, heat oil in a skillet and add ginger, onion, and garlic.
9. Sauté for 5 minutes, then add all the remaining ingredients.
10. Cook the mixture for 15 minutes approximately until well thoroughly mixed.
11. Serve the brisket with this sauce on top.

Nutrition:
- (Per serving) Calories 374 | Fat 25g |Sodium 275mg | Carbs 7.3g | Fiber 0g | Sugar 6g | Protein 12.3g

Lamb Shank With Mushroom Sauce

Servings: 4
Cooking Time: 35 Minutes.
Ingredients:
- 20 mushrooms, chopped
- 2 red bell pepper, chopped
- 2 red onion, chopped
- 1 cup red wine
- 4 leeks, chopped
- 6 tablespoons balsamic vinegar
- 2 teaspoons black pepper
- 2 teaspoons salt
- 3 tablespoons fresh rosemary
- 6 garlic cloves
- 4 lamb shanks
- 3 tablespoons olive oil

Directions:
1. Season the lamb shanks with salt, pepper, rosemary, and 1 teaspoon of olive oil.
2. Set half of the shanks in each of the crisper plate.
3. Return the crisper plate to the Ninja Foodi Dual Zone Air Fryer.
4. Choose the Air Fry mode for Zone 1 and set the temperature to 390 degrees F and the time to 25 minutes.
5. Select the "MATCH" button to copy the settings for Zone 2.
6. Initiate cooking by pressing the START/STOP button.
7. Flip the shanks halfway through, and resume cooking.
8. Meanwhile, add and heat the remaining olive oil in a skillet.
9. Add onion and garlic to sauté for 5 minutes.
10. Add in mushrooms and cook for 5 minutes.
11. Add red wine and cook until it is absorbed
12. Stir all the remaining vegetables along with black pepper and salt.
13. Cook until vegetables are al dente.
14. Serve the air fried shanks with sautéed vegetable fry.

Nutrition:
- (Per serving) Calories 352 | Fat 9.1g | Sodium 1294mg | Carbs 3.9g | Fiber 1g | Sugar 1g | Protein 61g

Tomahawk Steak

Servings: 4
Cooking Time: 12 Minutes
Ingredients:
- 4 tablespoons butter, softened
- 2 cloves garlic, minced
- 2 teaspoons chopped fresh parsley
- 1 teaspoon chopped chives
- 1 teaspoon chopped fresh thyme
- 1 teaspoon chopped fresh rosemary
- 2 (2 pounds each) bone-in ribeye steaks
- Kosher salt, to taste
- Freshly ground black pepper, to taste

Directions:
1. In a small bowl, combine the butter and herbs. Place the mixture in the center of a piece of plastic wrap and roll it into a log. Twist the ends together to keep it tight and refrigerate until hardened, about 20 minutes.
2. Season the steaks on both sides with salt and pepper.
3. Install a crisper plate in both drawers. Place one steak in the zone 1 drawer and one in zone 2's, then insert the drawers into the unit.
4. Select zone 1, select AIR FRY, set temperature to 390 degrees F/ 200 degrees C, and set time to 12 minutes. Select MATCH to match zone 2 settings to zone 1. Press the START/STOP button to begin cooking.
5. When the time reaches 10 minutes, press START/STOP to pause the unit. Remove the drawers and flip the steaks. Add the herb-butter to the tops of the steaks. Re-insert the drawers into the unit and press START/STOP to resume cooking.
6. Serve and enjoy!

Nutrition:
- (Per serving) Calories 338 | Fat 21.2g | Sodium 1503mg | Carbs 5.1g | Fiber 0.3g | Sugar 4.6g | Protein 29.3g

Beef Kofta Kebab

Servings: 4
Cooking Time: 20 Minutes
Ingredients:
- 455g ground beef
- ¼ cup white onion, grated
- ¼ cup parsley, chopped
- 1 tablespoon mint, chopped
- 2 cloves garlic, minced
- 1 teaspoon salt
- ½ teaspoon cumin
- 1 teaspoon oregano
- ½ teaspoon garlic salt
- 1 egg

Directions:
1. Mix ground beef with onion, parsley, mint, garlic, cumin, oregano, garlic salt and egg in a bowl.
2. Take 3 tbsp-sized beef kebabs out of this mixture.
3. Place the kebabs in the air fryer baskets.
4. Return the air fryer basket 1 to Zone 1, and basket 2 to Zone 2 of the Ninja Foodi 2-Basket Air Fryer.
5. Choose the "Air Fry" mode for Zone 1 at 375 degrees F and 18 minutes of cooking time.
6. Select the "MATCH COOK" option to copy the settings for Zone 2.
7. Initiate cooking by pressing the START/PAUSE BUTTON.
8. Flip the kebabs once cooked halfway through.
9. Serve warm.

Beef Ribs Ii

Servings: 2
Cooking Time: 1
Ingredients:
- ¼ cup olive oil
- 4 garlic cloves, minced
- ½ cup white wine vinegar
- ¼ cup soy sauce, reduced-sodium
- ¼ cup Worcestershire sauce
- 1 lemon juice
- Salt and black pepper, to taste
- 2 tablespoons of Italian seasoning
- 1 teaspoon of smoked paprika
- 2 tablespoons of mustard
- ½ cup maple syrup
- Meat Ingredients:
- Oil spray, for greasing
- 8 beef ribs lean

Directions:
1. Take a large bowl and add all the ingredients under marinade ingredients.
2. Put the marinade in a zip lock bag and add ribs to it.
3. Let it sit for 4 hours.
4. Now take out the basket of air fryer and grease the baskets with oil spray.
5. Now dived the ribs among two baskets.
6. Set it to AIR fry mode at 220 degrees F for 30 minutes.
7. Select Pause and take out the baskets.
8. Afterward, flip the ribs and cook for 30 minutes at 250 degrees F.
9. Once done, serve the juicy and tender ribs.
10. Enjoy.

Nutrition:
- (Per serving) Calories 1927| Fat116g| Sodium 1394mg | Carbs 35.2g | Fiber 1.3g| Sugar29 g | Protein 172.3g

Bacon-wrapped Filet Mignon

Servings: 4
Cooking Time: 15 Minutes
Ingredients:
- 4 bacon slices
- 4 (4-ounce) filet mignon
- Salt and ground black pepper, as required
- Olive oil cooking spray

Directions:
1. Wrap 1 bacon slice around each filet mignon and secure with toothpicks.
2. Spray the filet mignon with cooking spray evenly. Season the filets with salt and black pepper lightly.
3. Grease each basket of "Zone 1" and "Zone 2" of Ninja Foodi 2-Basket Air Fryer.
4. Press "Zone 1" and "Zone 2" and then rotate the knob for each zone to select "Air Fry".
5. Set the temperature to 400 degrees F/ 200 degrees C for both zones and then set the time for 5 minutes to preheat.
6. After preheating, arrange 2 filets into the basket of each zone.
7. Slide each basket into Air Fryer and set the time for 15 minutes.
8. While cooking, flip the filets once halfway through.
9. After cooking time is completed, remove the filets from Air Fryer and serve hot.

Cinnamon-apple Pork Chops

Servings: 4
Cooking Time: 10 Minutes
Ingredients:
- 2 tablespoons butter
- 4 boneless pork loin chops
- 3 tablespoons brown sugar
- 1 teaspoon ground cinnamon
- ½ teaspoon ground nutmeg
- ¼ teaspoon salt
- 4 medium tart apples, sliced
- 2 tablespoons chopped pecans

Directions:
1. Mix butter, brown sugar, cinnamon, nutmeg, and salt in a bowl.
2. Rub this mixture over the pork chops and place them in the air fryer baskets.
3. Top them with apples and pecans.
4. Return the air fryer basket 1 to Zone 1, and basket 2 to Zone 2 of the Ninja Foodi 2-Basket Air Fryer.
5. Choose the "Air Fry" mode for Zone 1 at 375 degrees F and 10 minutes of cooking time.
6. Select the "MATCH COOK" option to copy the settings for Zone 2.
7. Initiate cooking by pressing the START/PAUSE BUTTON.
8. Serve warm.

Yogurt Lamb Chops

Servings: 2
Cooking Time: 20
Ingredients:
- 1½ cups plain Greek yogurt
- 1 lemon, juice only
- 1 teaspoon ground cumin
- 1 teaspoon ground coriander
- ¾ teaspoon ground turmeric
- ¼ teaspoon ground allspice
- 10 rib lamb chops (1–1¼ inches thick cut)
- 2 tablespoons olive oil, divided

Directions:
1. Take a bowl and add lamb chop along with listed ingredients.
2. Rub the lamb chops well.
3. and let it marinate in the refrigerator for 1 hour.
4. Afterward takeout the lamb chops from the refrigerator.
5. Layer parchment paper on top of the baskets of the air fryer.
6. Divide it between ninja air fryer baskets.
7. Set the time for zone 1 to 20 minutes at 400 degrees F.
8. Select the MATCH button for the zone 2 basket.
9. Hit start and then wait for the chop to be cooked.
10. Once the cooking is done, the cool sign will appear on display.
11. Take out the lamb chops and let the chops serve on plates.

Nutrition:
- (Per serving) Calories 1973 | Fat 90 g| Sodium 228 mg | Carbs 109.2g | Fiber 1g | Sugar 77.5g | Protein 184g

Bbq Pork Spare Ribs

Servings: 8
Cooking Time: 30 Minutes
Ingredients:
- ½ cup honey, divided
- 1½ cups BBQ sauce
- 4 tablespoons tomato ketchup
- 2 tablespoons Worcestershire sauce
- 2 tablespoons low-sodium soy sauce
- 1 teaspoon garlic powder
- Freshly ground white pepper, as required
- 3½ pounds pork ribs

Directions:
1. In a bowl, mix together 6 tablespoons of honey and the remaining ingredients except pork ribs.
2. Add the pork ribs and coat with the mixture generously.
3. Refrigerate to marinate for about 20 minutes.
4. Grease each basket of "Zone 1" and "Zone 2" of Ninja Foodi 2-Basket Air Fryer.
5. Press "Zone 1" and "Zone 2" and then rotate the knob for each zone to select "Air Fry".
6. Set the temperature to 355 degrees F/ 180 degrees C for both zones and then set the time for 5 minutes to preheat.
7. After preheating, arrange the ribs into the basket of each zone.
8. Slide each basket into Air Fryer and set the time for 26 minutes.
9. While cooking, flip the ribs once halfway through.
10. After cooking time is completed, remove the ribs from Air Fryer and place onto serving plates.
11. Drizzle with the remaining honey and serve immediately.

Poultry Recipes

Simply Terrific Turkey Meatballs

Servings: 4
Cooking Time: 7 To 10 Minutes
Ingredients:
- 1 red bell pepper, seeded and coarsely chopped
- 2 cloves garlic, coarsely chopped
- 15 g chopped fresh parsley
- 680 g 85% lean turkey mince
- 1 egg, lightly beaten
- 45 g grated Parmesan cheese
- 1 teaspoon salt
- ½ teaspoon freshly ground black pepper

Directions:
1. Preheat the air fryer to 200°C.
2. In a food processor fitted with a metal blade, combine the bell pepper, garlic, and parsley. Pulse until finely chopped. Transfer the vegetables to a large mixing bowl.
3. Add the turkey, egg, Parmesan, salt, and black pepper. Mix gently until thoroughly combined. Shape the mixture into 1¼-inch meatballs.
4. Arrange the meatballs in a single layer in the two air fryer drawers; coat lightly with olive oil spray. Pausing halfway through the cooking time to shake the drawer, air fry for 7 to 10 minutes, until lightly browned and a thermometer inserted into the centre of a meatball registers 76°C.

Honey Butter Chicken

Servings: 4
Cooking Time: 15 Minutes
Ingredients:
- 4 chicken breasts, boneless
- 85g honey
- 28g butter, melted
- 2 tsp lemon juice
- 15ml olive oil
- 62g Dijon mustard
- Pepper
- Salt

Directions:
1. In a small bowl, mix butter, oil, lemon juice, honey, mustard, pepper, and salt.
2. Insert a crisper plate in the Ninja Foodi air fryer baskets.
3. Brush chicken breasts with butter mixture and place them in both baskets.
4. Select zone 1 then select "bake" mode and set the temperature to 380 degrees F for 15 minutes. Press "match" to match zone 2 settings to zone 1. Press "start/stop" to begin.

Nutrition:
- (Per serving) Calories 434 | Fat 20.7g |Sodium 384mg | Carbs 18.4g | Fiber 0.6g | Sugar 17.6g | Protein 43.1g

Chicken Bites

Servings: 4
Cooking Time: 20 Minutes
Ingredients:
- 900g chicken thighs, cut into chunks
- ¼ tsp white pepper
- ½ tsp onion powder
- 30ml olive oil
- 59ml fresh lemon juice
- ½ tsp garlic powder
- Pepper
- Salt

Directions:
1. Add chicken chunks and remaining ingredients into the bowl and mix well.
2. Cover the bowl and place it in the refrigerator overnight.
3. Insert a crisper plate in the Ninja Foodi air fryer baskets.
4. Place the marinated chicken in both baskets.
5. Select zone 1 then select "air fry" mode and set the temperature to 380 degrees F for 20 minutes. Press "match" to match zone 2 settings to zone 1. Press "start/stop" to begin.

Nutrition:
- (Per serving) Calories 497 | Fat 23.9g |Sodium 237mg | Carbs 0.9g | Fiber 0.2g | Sugar 0.5g | Protein 65.8g

Chicken And Vegetable Fajitas

Servings: 6
Cooking Time: 23 Minutes
Ingredients:
- Chicken:
- 450 g boneless, skinless chicken thighs, cut crosswise into thirds
- 1 tablespoon vegetable oil
- 4½ teaspoons taco seasoning
- Vegetables:
- 50 g sliced onion
- 150 g sliced bell pepper
- 1 or 2 jalapeños, quartered lengthwise
- 1 tablespoon vegetable oil
- ½ teaspoon kosher salt
- ½ teaspoon ground cumin
- For Serving:
- Tortillas
- Sour cream
- Shredded cheese
- Guacamole
- Salsa

Directions:
1. For the chicken: In a medium bowl, toss together the chicken, vegetable oil, and taco seasoning to coat. 2. For the vegetables: In a separate bowl, toss together the onion, bell pepper, jalapeño, vegetable oil, salt, and cumin to coat. 3. Place the chicken in the air fryer basket. Set the air fryer to (190°C for 10 minutes. Add the vegetables to the basket, toss everything together to blend the seasonings, and set the air fryer for 13 minutes more. Use a meat thermometer to ensure the chicken has reached an internal temperature of 75°C. 4. Transfer the chicken and vegetables to a serving platter. Serve with tortillas and the desired fajita fixings.

Air-fried Turkey Breast With Roasted Green Bean Casserole

Servings: 4
Cooking Time: 50 Minutes
Ingredients:
- FOR THE TURKEY BREAST
- 2 teaspoons unsalted butter, at room temperature
- 1 bone-in split turkey breast (3 pounds), thawed if frozen
- 1 teaspoon poultry seasoning
- ½ teaspoon kosher salt
- ⅓ teaspoon freshly ground black pepper
- FOR THE GREEN BEAN CASSEROLE
- 1 (10.5-ounce) can condensed cream of mushroom soup
- ½ cup whole milk
- 1 cup store-bought crispy fried onions, divided
- ¼ teaspoon kosher salt
- ¼ teaspoon freshly ground black pepper
- 1 pound green beans, trimmed
- ¼ cup panko bread crumbs
- Nonstick cooking spray

Directions:
1. To prep the turkey breast: Spread the butter over the skin side of the turkey. Season with the poultry seasoning, salt, and black pepper.
2. To prep the green bean casserole: In a medium bowl, combine the soup, milk, ½ cup of crispy onions, the salt, and black pepper.
3. To cook the turkey and beans:
4. Install a crisper plate in the Zone 1 basket. Place the turkey skin-side up in the basket and insert the basket in the unit. Place the green beans in the Zone 2 basket and insert the basket in the unit.
5. Select Zone 1, select AIR FRY, set the temperature to 360°F, and set the time to 50 minutes.
6. Select Zone 2, select ROAST, set the temperature to 350°F, and set the time to 40 minutes. Select SMART FINISH.
7. Press START/PAUSE to begin cooking.
8. When the Zone 2 timer reads 30 minutes, press START/PAUSE. Remove the basket and stir the soup mixture into the beans. Scatter the panko and remaining ½ cup of crispy onions over the top, then spritz with cooking spray. Reinsert the basket and press START/PAUSE to resume cooking.
9. When cooking is complete, the turkey will be cooked through and the green bean casserole will be bubbling and golden brown on top.
10. Let the turkey and casserole rest for at least 15 minutes before serving.
11. Per serving
12. Calories: 577| Total fat: 22g| Saturated fat: 6.5g| Carbohydrates: 24g| Fiber: 3.5g| Protein: 68g| Sodium: 1,165mg

Greek Chicken Souvlaki

Servings: 3 To 4
Cooking Time: 15 Minutes
Ingredients:
- Chicken:
- Grated zest and juice of 1 lemon
- 2 tablespoons extra-virgin olive oil
- 1 tablespoon Greek souvlaki seasoning
- 450 g boneless, skinless chicken breast, cut into 2-inch chunks
- Vegetable oil spray
- For Serving:
- Warm pita bread or hot cooked rice
- Sliced ripe tomatoes
- Sliced cucumbers
- Thinly sliced red onion
- Kalamata olives
- Tzatziki

Directions:
1. For the chicken: In a small bowl, combine the lemon zest, lemon juice, olive oil, and souvlaki seasoning. Place the chicken in a gallon-size resealable plastic bag. Pour the marinade over chicken. Seal bag and massage to coat. Place the bag in a large bowl and marinate for 30 minutes, or cover and refrigerate up to 24 hours, turning the bag occasionally. 2. Place the chicken a single layer in the zone 1 air fryer drawer. Cook at 180°C for 10 minutes, turning the chicken and spraying with a little vegetable oil spray halfway through the cooking time. Increase the air fryer temperature to 200°C for 5 minutes to allow the chicken to crisp and brown a little. 3. Transfer the chicken to a serving platter and serve with pita bread or rice, tomatoes, cucumbers, onion, olives and tzatziki.

Bacon-wrapped Chicken

Servings: 2
Cooking Time: 28 Minutes
Ingredients:
- Butter:
- ½ stick butter softened
- ½ garlic clove, minced
- ¼ teaspoon dried thyme
- ¼ teaspoon dried basil
- ⅛ teaspoon coarse salt
- 1 pinch black pepper, ground
- ⅓ lb. thick-cut bacon
- 1 ½ lbs. boneless skinless chicken thighs
- 2 teaspoons garlic, minced

Directions:
1. Mix garlic softened butter with thyme, salt, basil, and black pepper in a bowl.
2. Add butter mixture on a piece of wax paper and roll it up tightly to make a butter log.
3. Place the log in the refrigerator for 2 hours.
4. Spray one bacon strip on a piece of wax paper.
5. Place each chicken thigh on top of one bacon strip and rub it with garlic.
6. Make a slit in the chicken thigh and add a teaspoon of butter to the chicken.
7. Wrap the bacon around the chicken thigh.
8. Repeat those same steps with all the chicken thighs.
9. Place the bacon-wrapped chicken thighs in the two crisper plates.
10. Return the crisper plates to the Ninja Foodi Dual Zone Air Fryer.
11. Choose the Air Fry mode for Zone 1 and set the temperature to 390 degrees F and the time to 28 minutes|
12. Select the "MATCH" button to copy the settings for Zone 2.
13. Initiate cooking by pressing the START/STOP button.
14. Flip the chicken once cooked halfway through, and resume cooking.
15. Serve warm.

Chipotle Drumsticks

Servings: 4
Cooking Time: 20 Minutes
Ingredients:
- 1 tablespoon tomato paste
- ½ teaspoon chipotle powder
- ¼ teaspoon apple cider vinegar
- ¼ teaspoon garlic powder
- 8 chicken drumsticks
- ½ teaspoon salt
- ⅛ teaspoon ground black pepper

Directions:
1. In a small bowl, combine tomato paste, chipotle powder, vinegar, and garlic powder.
2. Sprinkle drumsticks with salt and pepper, then place into a large bowl and pour in tomato paste mixture. Toss or stir to evenly coat all drumsticks in mixture.
3. Place drumsticks into two ungreased air fryer baskets. Adjust the temperature to 200°C and air fry for 25 minutes, turning drumsticks halfway through cooking. Drumsticks will be dark red with an internal temperature of at least 75°C when done. Serve warm.

Greek Chicken Meatballs

Servings: 4
Cooking Time: 9 Minutes
Ingredients:
- 455g ground chicken
- 1 large egg
- 1½ tablespoons garlic paste
- 1 tablespoon dried oregano
- 1 teaspoon lemon zest
- 1 teaspoon dried onion powder
- ¾ teaspoon salt
- ¼ teaspoon black pepper
- Oil spray

Directions:
1. Mix ground chicken with rest of the ingredients in a bowl.
2. Make 1-inch sized meatballs out of this mixture.
3. Place the meatballs in the air fryer baskets.
4. Return the air fryer basket 1 to Zone 1, and basket 2 to Zone 2 of the Ninja Foodi 2-Basket Air Fryer.
5. Choose the "Air Fry" mode for Zone 1 and set the temperature to 390 degrees F and 9 minutes of cooking time.
6. Select the "MATCH COOK" option to copy the settings for Zone 2.
7. Initiate cooking by pressing the START/PAUSE BUTTON.
8. Serve warm.

Nutrition:
- (Per serving) Calories 346 | Fat 16.1g | Sodium 882mg | Carbs 1.3g | Fiber 0.5g | Sugar 0.5g | Protein 48.2g

Honey-glazed Chicken Thighs

Servings: 4
Cooking Time: 14 Minutes
Ingredients:
- Oil, for spraying
- 4 boneless, skinless chicken thighs, fat trimmed
- 3 tablespoons soy sauce
- 1 tablespoon balsamic vinegar
- 2 teaspoons honey
- 2 teaspoons minced garlic
- 1 teaspoon ground ginger

Directions:
1. Preheat the zone 1 air fryer drawer to 200°C. Line the zone 1 air fryer drawer with parchment and spray lightly with oil.
2. Place the chicken in the prepared drawer.
3. Cook for 7 minutes, flip, and cook for another 7 minutes, or until the internal temperature reaches 76°C and the juices run clear.
4. In a small saucepan, combine the soy sauce, balsamic vinegar, honey, garlic, and ginger and cook over low heat for 1 to 2 minutes, until warmed through.
5. Transfer the chicken to a serving plate and drizzle with the sauce just before serving.

Chicken And Potatoes

Servings: 2
Cooking Time: 10 Minutes
Ingredients:
- 2 potatoes, diced
- 2 chicken breasts, diced
- 4 cloves garlic crushed
- 2 teaspoons smoked paprika
- ½ teaspoon red chili flakes
- 1 teaspoon fresh thyme
- 1 teaspoon salt
- ¼ teaspoon black pepper
- 2 tablespoons olive oil

Directions:
1. Rub chicken with half of the salt, black pepper, oil, thyme, red chili flakes, paprika and garlic.
2. Mix potatoes with remaining spices, oil and garlic in a bowl.
3. Add chicken to one air fryer basket and potatoes the second basket.
4. Return the air fryer basket 1 to Zone 1, and basket 2 to Zone 2 of the Ninja Foodi 2-Basket Air Fryer.
5. Choose the "Air Fry" mode for Zone 1 at 375 degrees F and 10 minutes of cooking time.
6. Select the "MATCH COOK" option to copy the settings for Zone 2.
7. Initiate cooking by pressing the START/PAUSE BUTTON.
8. Flip the chicken and toss potatoes once cooked halfway through.
9. Garnish with chopped parsley.
10. Serve chicken with the potatoes.

Nutrition:
- (Per serving) Calories 374 | Fat 13g | Sodium 552mg | Carbs 25g | Fiber 1.2g | Sugar 1.2g | Protein 37.7g

Cornish Hen With Asparagus

Servings: 2
Cooking Time: 45
Ingredients:
- 10 spears of asparagus
- Salt and black pepper, to taste
- 1 Cornish hen
- Salt, to taste
- Black pepper, to taste
- 1 teaspoon of Paprika
- Coconut spray, for greasing
- 2 lemons, sliced

Directions:
1. Wash and pat dry the asparagus and coat it with coconut oil spray.
2. Sprinkle salt on the asparagus and place inside the first basket of the air fryer.
3. Next, take the Cornish hen and rub it well with the salt, black pepper, and paprika.
4. Oil sprays the Cornish hen and place in the second air fryer basket.
5. Press button 1 for the first basket and set it to AIR FRY mode at 350 degrees F, for 8 minutes.
6. For the second basket hit 2 and set the time to 45 minutes at 350 degrees F, by selecting the ROAST mode.
7. To start cooking, hit the smart finish button and press hit start.
8. Once the 6 minutes pass press 1 and pause and take out the asparagus.
9. Once the chicken cooking cycle complete, press 2 and hit pause.
10. Take out the Basket of chicken and let it transfer to the serving plate
11. Serve the chicken with roasted asparagus and slices of lemon.
12. Serve hot and enjoy.

Nutrition:
- (Per serving) Calories 192| Fat 4.7g| Sodium 151mg | Carbs10.7 g | Fiber 4.6g | Sugar 3.8g | Protein 30g

Chicken Thighs In Waffles

Servings: 4
Cooking Time: 40 Minutes
Ingredients:
- For the chicken:
- 4 chicken thighs, skin on
- 240 ml low-fat buttermilk
- 65 g all-purpose flour
- ½ teaspoon garlic powder
- ½ teaspoon mustard powder
- 1 teaspoon kosher salt
- ½ teaspoon freshly ground black pepper
- 85 g honey, for serving
- Cooking spray
- For the waffles:
- 65 g all-purpose flour
- 65 g whole wheat pastry flour
- 1 large egg, beaten
- 240 ml low-fat buttermilk
- 1 teaspoon baking powder
- 2 tablespoons rapeseed oil
- ½ teaspoon kosher salt
- 1 tablespoon granulated sugar

Directions:
1. Combine the chicken thighs with buttermilk in a large bowl. Wrap the bowl in plastic and refrigerate to marinate for at least an hour. 2. Preheat the air fryer to 180ºC. Spritz the two air fryer baskets with cooking spray. 3. Combine the flour, mustard powder, garlic powder, salt, and black pepper in a shallow dish. Stir to mix well. 4. Remove the thighs from the buttermilk and pat dry with paper towels. Sit the bowl of buttermilk aside. 5. Dip the thighs in the flour mixture first, then into the buttermilk, and then into the flour mixture. Shake the excess off. 6. Arrange the thighs in the two preheated air fryer baskets and spritz with cooking spray. Air fryer for 20 minutes or until an instant-read thermometer inserted in the thickest part of the chicken thighs registers at least 75ºC. Flip the thighs halfway through. 7. Meanwhile, make the waffles: combine the ingredients for the waffles in a large bowl. Stir to mix well, then arrange the mixture in a waffle iron and cook until a golden and fragrant waffle forms. 8. Remove the waffles from the waffle iron and slice into 4 pieces. Remove the chicken thighs from the air fryer and allow to cool for 5 minutes. 9. Arrange each chicken thigh on each waffle piece and drizzle with 1 tablespoon of honey. Serve warm.

Wings With Corn On The Cob

Servings: 2
Cooking Time: 40 Minutes
Ingredients:
- 6 chicken wings, skinless
- 2 tablespoons coconut amino
- 2 tablespoons brown sugar
- 1 teaspoon ginger, paste
- ½ inch garlic, minced
- Salt and black pepper to taste
- 2 corn on cobs, small
- Oil spray, for greasing

Directions:
1. Spray the corns with oil spray and season them with salt.
2. Coat the chicken wings with coconut amino, brown sugar, ginger, garlic, salt, and black pepper.
3. Spray the wings with a good amount of oil spray.
4. Put the chicken wings in the zone 1 basket.
5. Put the corn into the zone 2 basket.
6. Select ROAST mode for the chicken wings and set the time to 23 minutes at 400 degrees F/ 200 degrees C.
7. Press 2 and select the AIR FRY mode for the corn and set the time to 40 at 300 degrees F/ 150 degrees C.
8. Once it's done, serve and enjoy.

Nutrition:
- (Per serving) Calories 950 | Fat 33.4g | Sodium 592 mg | Carbs 27.4g | Fiber 2.1g | Sugar 11.3 g | Protein 129g

Sesame Ginger Chicken

Servings: 4
Cooking Time: 30 Minutes
Ingredients:
- 4 ounces green beans
- 1 tablespoon canola oil
- 1½ pounds boneless, skinless chicken breasts
- ⅓ cup prepared sesame-ginger sauce
- Kosher salt, to taste
- Black pepper, to taste

Directions:
1. Toss the green beans with a teaspoon of salt and pepper in a medium mixing bowl.
2. Place a crisper plate in each drawer. Place the green beans in the zone 1 drawer and insert it into the unit. Place the chicken breasts in the zone 2 drawer and place it inside the unit.
3. Select zone 1, then AIR FRY, and set the temperature to 390 degrees F/ 200 degrees C with a 10-minute timer. Select zone 2, then AIR FRY, and set the temperature to 390 degrees F/ 200 degrees C with an 18-minute timer. Select SYNC. To begin cooking, press the START/STOP button.
4. Press START/STOP to pause the unit when the zone 2 timer reaches 9 minutes. Remove the chicken from the drawer and toss it in the sesame ginger sauce. To resume cooking, re-insert the drawer into the unit and press START/STOP.
5. When cooking is complete, serve the chicken breasts and green beans straight away.

Nutrition:
- (Per serving) Calories 143 | Fat 7g | Sodium 638mg | Carbs 11.6g | Fiber 1.4g | Sugar 8.5g | Protein 11.1g

Balsamic Duck Breast

Servings: 2
Cooking Time: 20 Minutes
Ingredients:
- 2 duck breasts
- 1 teaspoon parsley
- Salt and black pepper, to taste
- Marinade:
- 1 tablespoon olive oil
- ½ teaspoon French mustard
- 1 teaspoon dried garlic
- 2 teaspoons honey
- ½ teaspoon balsamic vinegar

Directions:
1. Mix olive oil, mustard, garlic, honey, and balsamic vinegar in a bowl.
2. Add duck breasts to the marinade and rub well.
3. Place one duck breast in each crisper plate.
4. Return the crisper plates to the Ninja Foodi Dual Zone Air Fryer.
5. Choose the Air Fry mode for Zone 1 and set the temperature to 360 degrees F and the time to 20 minutes|
6. Select the "MATCH" button to copy the settings for Zone 2.
7. Initiate cooking by pressing the START/STOP button.
8. Flip the duck breasts once cooked halfway through, then resume cooking.
9. Serve warm.

Whole Chicken

Servings: 8
Cooking Time: 20 Minutes
Ingredients:
- 1 whole chicken (about 2.8 pounds), cut in half
- 4 tablespoons olive oil
- 2 teaspoons paprika
- 1 teaspoon garlic powder
- 1 teaspoon onion powder
- Salt and pepper, to taste

Directions:
1. Mix the olive oil, paprika, garlic powder, and onion powder together in a bowl.
2. Place the chicken halves, breast side up, on a plate. Spread a teaspoon or two of the oil mix all over the halves using either your hands or a brush. Season with salt and pepper.
3. Flip the chicken halves over and repeat on the other side. You'll want to reserve a little of the oil mix for later, but other than that, use it liberally.
4. Install a crisper plate in both drawers. Place one half of the chicken in the zone 1 drawer and the other half in the zone 2 drawer, then insert the drawers into the unit.
5. Select zone 1, select AIR FRY, set temperature to 390 degrees F/ 200 degrees C, and set time to 20 minutes. Select MATCH to match zone 2 settings to zone 1. Press the START/STOP button to begin cooking.
6. When cooking is done, check the internal temperature of the chicken. It should read 165°F. If the chicken isn't done, add more cooking time.

Nutrition:
- (Per serving) Calories 131 | Fat 8g | Sodium 51mg | Carbs 0g | Fiber 0g | Sugar 0g | Protein 14g

Fajita Chicken Strips & Barbecued Chicken With Creamy Coleslaw

Servings: 6
Cooking Time: 20 Minutes
Ingredients:
- Fajita Chicken Strips:
- 450 g boneless, skinless chicken tenderloins, cut into strips
- 3 bell peppers, any color, cut into chunks
- 1 onion, cut into chunks
- 1 tablespoon olive oil
- 1 tablespoon fajita seasoning mix
- Cooking spray
- Barbecued Chicken with Creamy Coleslaw:
- 270 g shredded coleslaw mix
- Salt and pepper
- 2 (340 g) bone-in split chicken breasts, trimmed
- 1 teaspoon vegetable oil
- 2 tablespoons barbecue sauce, plus extra for serving
- 2 tablespoons mayonnaise
- 2 tablespoons sour cream
- 1 teaspoon distilled white vinegar, plus extra for seasoning
- ¼ teaspoon sugar

Directions:
1. Make the Fajita Chicken Strips :
2. Preheat the air fryer to 190°C.
3. In a large bowl, mix together the chicken, bell peppers, onion, olive oil, and fajita seasoning mix until completely coated.
4. Spray the zone 1 air fryer basket lightly with cooking spray.
5. Place the chicken and vegetables in the zone 1 air fryer basket and lightly spray with cooking spray.
6. Air fry for 7 minutes. Shake the basket and air fry for an additional 5 to 8 minutes, until the chicken is cooked through and the veggies are starting to char.
7. Serve warm.
8. Make the Barbecued Chicken with Creamy Coleslaw :
9. Preheat the air fryer to 180°C.
10. Toss coleslaw mix and ¼ teaspoon salt in a colander set over bowl. Let sit until wilted slightly, about 30 minutes. Rinse, drain, and dry well with a dish towel.
11. Meanwhile, pat chicken dry with paper towels, rub with oil, and season with salt and pepper. Arrange breasts skin-side down in zone 2 air fryer basket, spaced evenly apart, alternating ends. Bake for 10 minutes. Flip breasts and brush skin side with barbecue sauce. Return basket to air fryer and bake until well browned and chicken registers 70°C, 10 to 15 minutes.
12. Transfer chicken to serving platter, tent loosely with aluminum foil, and let rest for 5 minutes. While chicken rests, whisk mayonnaise, sour cream, vinegar, sugar, and pinch pepper together in a large bowl. Stir in coleslaw mix and season with salt, pepper, and additional vinegar to taste. Serve chicken with coleslaw, passing extra barbecue sauce separately.

Crispy Dill Chicken Strips

Servings: 4
Cooking Time: 10 Minutes
Ingredients:
- 2 whole boneless, skinless chicken breasts (about 450 g each), halved lengthwise
- 230 ml Italian dressing
- 110 g finely crushed crisps
- 1 tablespoon dried dill weed
- 1 tablespoon garlic powder
- 1 large egg, beaten
- 1 to 2 tablespoons oil

Directions:
1. In a large resealable bag, combine the chicken and Italian dressing. Seal the bag and refrigerate to marinate at least 1 hour.
2. In a shallow dish, stir together the potato chips, dill, and garlic powder. Place the beaten egg in a second shallow dish.
3. Remove the chicken from the marinade. Roll the chicken pieces in the egg and the crisp mixture, coating thoroughly.
4. Preheat the air fryer to 170°C. Line the two air fryer drawers with parchment paper.
5. Place the coated chicken on the parchment and spritz with oil.
6. Cook for 5 minutes. Flip the chicken, spritz it with oil, and cook for 5 minutes more until the outsides are crispy and the insides are no longer pink.

Almond Chicken

Servings: 4
Cooking Time: 25 Minutes
Ingredients:
- 2 large eggs
- ½ cup buttermilk
- 2 teaspoons garlic salt
- 1 teaspoon pepper
- 2 cups slivered almonds, finely chopped
- 4 boneless, skinless chicken breast halves (6 ounces each)

Directions:
1. Whisk together the egg, buttermilk, garlic salt, and pepper in a small bowl.
2. In another small bowl, place the almonds.
3. Dip the chicken in the egg mixture, then roll it in the almonds, patting it down to help the coating stick.
4. Install a crisper plate in both drawers. Place half the chicken breasts in the zone 1 drawer and half in zone 2's, then insert the drawers into the unit.
5. Select zone 1, select AIR FRY, set temperature to 390 degrees F/ 200 degrees C, and set time to 22 minutes. Select MATCH to match zone 2 settings to zone 1. Press the START/STOP button to begin cooking.
6. When the time reaches 11 minutes, press START/STOP to pause the unit. Remove the drawers and flip the chicken. Re-insert the drawers into the unit and press START/STOP to resume cooking.
7. When cooking is complete, remove the chicken.

Nutrition:
- (Per serving) Calories 353 | Fat 18g | Sodium 230mg | Carbs 6g | Fiber 2g | Sugar 3g | Protein 41g

Chicken Breast Strips

Servings: 2
Cooking Time: 22
Ingredients:
- 2 large organic egg
- 1-ounce buttermilk
- 1 cup of cornmeal
- ¼ cup all-purpose flour
- Salt and black pepper, to taste
- 1 pound of chicken breasts, cut into strips
- 2 tablespoons of oil bay seasoning
- oil spray, for greasing

Directions:
1. Take a medium bowl and whisk eggs with buttermilk.
2. In a separate large bowl mix flour, cornmeal, salt, black pepper, and oil bay seasoning.
3. First, dip the chicken breast strip in egg wash and then dredge into the flour mixture.
4. Coat the strip all over and layer on both the baskets that are already grease with oil spray.
5. Grease the chicken breast strips with oil spray as well.
6. Set the zone 1 basket to AIR FRY mode at 400 degrees F for 22 minutes.
7. Select the MATCH button for zone 2.
8. Hit the start button to let the cooking start.
9. Once the cooking cycle is done, serve.

Nutrition:
- (Per serving) Calories 788| Fat25g| Sodium835 mg | Carbs60g | Fiber 4.9g| Sugar1.5g | Protein79g

Glazed Thighs With French Fries

Servings: 3
Cooking Time: 35
Ingredients:
- 2 tablespoons of Soy Sauce
- Salt, to taste
- 1 teaspoon of Worcestershire Sauce
- 2 teaspoons Brown Sugar
- 1 teaspoon of Ginger, paste
- 1 teaspoon of Garlic, paste
- 6 Boneless Chicken Thighs
- 1 pound of hand-cut potato fries
- 2 tablespoons of canola oil

Directions:
1. Coat the French fries well with canola oil.
2. Season it with salt.
3. In a small bowl, combine the soy sauce, Worcestershire sauce, brown sugar, ginger, and garlic.
4. Place the chicken in this marinade and let it sit for 40 minutes.
5. Put the chicken thighs into the zone 1 basket and fries into the zone 2 basket.
6. Press button 1 for the first basket, and set it to ROAST mode at 350 degrees F for 35 minutes.
7. For the second basket hit 2 and set time to 30 minutes at 360 degrees F, by selecting AIR FRY mode.
8. Once the cooking cycle completely take out the fries and chicken and serve it hot.

Nutrition:
- (Per serving) Calories 858| Fat39g | Sodium 1509mg | Carbs 45.6g | Fiber 4.4g | Sugar3 g | Protein 90g

Roasted Garlic Chicken Pizza With Cauliflower "wings"

Servings: 4
Cooking Time: 25 Minutes
Ingredients:
- FOR THE PIZZA
- 2 prebaked rectangular pizza crusts or flatbreads
- 2 tablespoons olive oil
- 1 tablespoon minced garlic
- 1½ cups shredded part-skim mozzarella cheese
- 6 ounces boneless, skinless chicken breast, thinly sliced
- ¼ teaspoon red pepper flakes (optional)
- FOR THE CAULIFLOWER "WINGS"
- 4 cups cauliflower florets
- 1 tablespoon vegetable oil
- ½ cup Buffalo wing sauce

Directions:
1. To prep the pizza:
2. Trim the pizza crusts to fit in the air fryer basket, if necessary.
3. Brush the top of each crust with the oil and sprinkle with the garlic. Top the crusts with the mozzarella, chicken, and red pepper flakes .
4. To prep the cauliflower "wings": In a large bowl, combine the cauliflower and oil and toss to coat the florets.
5. To cook the pizza and "wings":
6. Install a crisper plate in each of the two baskets. Place one pizza in the Zone 1 basket and insert the basket in the unit. Place the cauliflower in the Zone 2 basket and insert the basket in the unit.
7. Select Zone 1, select ROAST, set the temperature to 375°F, and set the time to 25 minutes.
8. Select Zone 2, select AIR FRY, set the temperature to 390°F, and set the time to 25 minutes. Select SMART FINISH.
9. Press START/PAUSE to begin cooking.
10. When the Zone 1 timer reads 13 minutes, press START/PAUSE. Remove the basket. Transfer the pizza to a cutting board . Add the second pizza to the basket. Reinsert the basket in the unit and press START/PAUSE to resume cooking.
11. When the Zone 2 timer reads 5 minutes, press START/PAUSE. Remove the basket and add the Buffalo wing sauce to the cauliflower. Shake well to evenly coat the cauliflower in the sauce. Reinsert the basket and press START/PAUSE to resume cooking.
12. When cooking is complete, the cauliflower will be crisp on the outside and tender inside, and the chicken on the second pizza will be cooked through and the cheese melted.
13. Cut each pizza into 4 slices. Serve with the cauliflower "wings" on the side.

Crusted Chicken Breast

Servings: 4
Cooking Time: 28 Minutes
Ingredients:
- 2 large eggs, beaten
- ½ cup all-purpose flour
- 1 ¼ cups panko bread crumbs
- ⅔ cup Parmesan, grated
- 4 teaspoons lemon zest
- 2 teaspoons dried oregano
- Salt, to taste
- 1 teaspoon cayenne pepper
- Freshly black pepper, to taste
- 4 boneless skinless chicken breasts

Directions:
1. Beat eggs in one shallow bowl and spread flour in another shallow bowl.
2. Mix panko with oregano, lemon zest, Parmesan, cayenne, oregano, salt, and black pepper in another shallow bowl.
3. First, coat the chicken with flour first, then dip it in the eggs and coat them with panko mixture.
4. Arrange the prepared chicken in the two crisper plates.
5. Return the crisper plate to the Ninja Foodi Dual Zone Air Fryer.
6. Choose the Air Fry mode for Zone 1 and set the temperature to 390 degrees F and the time to 28 minutes
7. Select the "MATCH" button to copy the settings for Zone 2.
8. Initiate cooking by pressing the START/STOP button.
9. Flip the half-cooked chicken and continue cooking for 5 minutes until golden.
10. Serve warm.

"fried" Chicken With Warm Baked Potato Salad

Servings: 4
Cooking Time: 40 Minutes
Ingredients:
- FOR THE "FRIED" CHICKEN
- 1 cup buttermilk
- 1 tablespoon kosher salt
- 4 bone-in, skin-on chicken drumsticks and/or thighs
- 2 cups all-purpose flour
- 1 tablespoon seasoned salt
- 1 tablespoon paprika
- Nonstick cooking spray
- FOR THE POTATO SALAD
- 1½ pounds baby red potatoes, halved
- 1 tablespoon vegetable oil
- ½ cup mayonnaise
- ⅓ cup plain reduced-fat Greek yogurt
- 1 tablespoon apple cider vinegar
- ½ teaspoon kosher salt
- ½ teaspoon freshly ground black pepper
- ¾ cup shredded Cheddar cheese
- 4 slices cooked bacon, crumbled
- 3 scallions, sliced

Directions:
1. To prep the chicken:
2. In a large bowl, combine the buttermilk and salt. Add the chicken and turn to coat. Let rest for at least 30 minutes .
3. In a separate large bowl, combine the flour, seasoned salt, and paprika.
4. Remove the chicken from the marinade and allow any excess marinade to drip off. Discard the marinade. Dip the chicken pieces in the flour, coating them thoroughly. Mist with cooking spray. Let the chicken rest for 10 minutes.
5. To prep the potatoes: In a large bowl, combine the potatoes and oil and toss to coat.
6. To cook the chicken and potatoes:
7. Install a crisper plate in the Zone 1 basket. Place the chicken in the basket in a single layer and insert the basket in the unit. Place the potatoes in the Zone 2 basket and insert the basket in the unit.
8. Select Zone 1, select AIR FRY, set the temperature to 390°F, and set the time to 30 minutes.
9. Select Zone 2, select BAKE, set the temperature to 400°F, and set the time to 40 minutes. Select SMART FINISH.
10. Press START/PAUSE to begin cooking.
11. When cooking is complete, the chicken will be golden brown and cooked through and the potatoes will be fork-tender.
12. Rinse the potatoes under cold water for about 1 minute to cool them.
13. Place the potatoes in a large bowl and stir in the mayonnaise, yogurt, vinegar, salt, and black pepper. Gently stir in the Cheddar, bacon, and scallions. Serve warm with the "fried" chicken.

Brazilian Chicken Drumsticks

Servings: 6
Cooking Time: 47 Minutes
Ingredients:
- 2 teaspoons cumin seeds
- 2 teaspoons dried parsley
- 2 teaspoons turmeric powder
- 2 teaspoons dried oregano leaves
- 2 teaspoons salt
- 1 teaspoon coriander seeds
- 1 teaspoon black peppercorns
- 1 teaspoon cayenne pepper
- ½ cup lime juice
- 4 tablespoons vegetable oil
- 3 lbs. chicken drumsticks

Directions:
1. Grind cumin, parsley, salt, coriander seeds, cayenne pepper, peppercorns, oregano, and turmeric in a food processor.
2. Add this mixture to lemon juice and oil in a bowl and mix well.
3. Rub the spice paste over the chicken drumsticks and let them marinate for 30 minutes.
4. Divide the chicken drumsticks in both the crisper plates.
5. Return the crisper plates to the Ninja Foodi Dual Zone Air Fryer.
6. Choose the Air Fry mode for Zone 1 and set the temperature to 390 degrees F and the time to 47 minutes.
7. Select the "MATCH" button to copy the settings for Zone 2.
8. Initiate cooking by pressing the START/STOP button.
9. Flip the drumsticks when cooked halfway through, then resume cooking.
10. Serve warm.

Lemon-pepper Chicken Thighs With Buttery Roasted Radishes

Servings: 4
Cooking Time: 28 Minutes
Ingredients:
- FOR THE CHICKEN
- 4 bone-in, skin-on chicken thighs (6 ounces each)
- 1 teaspoon olive oil
- 2 teaspoons lemon pepper
- ¼ teaspoon kosher salt
- FOR THE RADISHES
- 1 bunch radishes (greens removed), halved through the stem
- 1 teaspoon olive oil
- ¼ teaspoon kosher salt
- ¼ teaspoon freshly ground black pepper
- 1 tablespoon unsalted butter, cut into small pieces
- 2 tablespoons chopped fresh parsley

Directions:
1. To prep the chicken: Brush both sides of the chicken thighs with olive oil, then season with lemon pepper and salt.
2. To prep the radishes: In a large bowl, combine the radishes, olive oil, salt, and black pepper. Stir well to coat the radishes.
3. To cook the chicken and radishes: Install a crisper plate in each of the two baskets. Place the chicken skin-side up in the Zone 1 basket and insert the basket in the unit. Place the radishes in the Zone 2 basket and insert the basket in the unit.
4. Select Zone 1, select AIR FRY, set the temperature to 390°F, and set the time to 28 minutes.
5. Select Zone 2, select ROAST, set the temperature to 400°F, and set the time to 15 minutes. Select SMART FINISH.
6. Press START/PAUSE to begin cooking.
7. When the Zone 2 timer reads 5 minutes, press START/PAUSE. Remove the basket, scatter the butter pieces over the radishes, and reinsert the basket. Press START/PAUSE to resume cooking.
8. When cooking is complete, the chicken should be cooked through and the radishes will be soft. Stir the parsley into the radishes and serve.

Chicken Parmesan

Servings: 4
Cooking Time: 10 Minutes
Ingredients:
- Oil, for spraying
- 2 (230 g) boneless, skinless chicken breasts
- 120 g Italian-style bread crumbs
- 20 g grated Parmesan cheese, plus 45 g shredded
- 4 tablespoons unsalted butter, melted
- 115 g marinara sauce

Directions:
1. Preheat the air fryer to 180°C. Line the two air fryer drawers with parchment and spray lightly with oil.
2. Cut each chicken breast in half through its thickness to make 4 thin cutlets. Using a meat tenderizer, pound each cutlet until it is about ¾ inch thick.
3. On a plate, mix together the bread crumbs and grated Parmesan cheese.
4. Lightly brush the chicken with the melted butter, then dip into the bread crumb mixture.
5. Place the chicken in the two prepared drawers and spray lightly with oil.
6. Cook for 6 minutes. Top the chicken with the marinara and shredded Parmesan cheese, dividing evenly. Cook for another 3 to 4 minutes, or until golden brown, crispy, and the internal temperature reaches 76°C.

Bang-bang Chicken

Servings: 2
Cooking Time: 20 Minutes
Ingredients:
- 1 cup mayonnaise
- ½ cup sweet chili sauce
- 2 tablespoons Sriracha sauce
- ⅓ cup flour
- 1 lb. boneless chicken breast, diced
- 1 ½ cups panko bread crumbs
- 2 green onions, chopped

Directions:
1. Mix mayonnaise with Sriracha and sweet chili sauce in a large bowl.
2. Keep ¾ cup of the mixture aside.
3. Add flour, chicken, breadcrumbs, and remaining mayo mixture to a resealable plastic bag.
4. Zip the bag and shake well to coat.
5. Divide the chicken in the two crisper plates in a single layer.
6. Return the crisper plate to the Ninja Foodi Dual Zone Air Fryer.
7. Choose the Air Fry mode for Zone 1 and set the temperature to 390 degrees F and the time to 20 minutes|
8. Select the "MATCH" button to copy the settings for Zone 2.
9. Initiate cooking by pressing the START/STOP button.
10. Flip the chicken once cooked halfway through.
11. Top the chicken with reserved mayo sauce.
12. Garnish with green onions and serve warm.

Cheddar-stuffed Chicken

Servings: 4
Cooking Time: 20 Minutes
Ingredients:
- 3 bacon strips, cooked and crumbled
- 2 ounces Cheddar cheese, cubed
- ¼ cup barbeque sauce
- 2 (4 ounces) boneless chicken breasts
- Salt and black pepper to taste

Directions:
1. Make a 1-inch deep pouch in each chicken breast.
2. Mix cheddar cubes with half of the BBQ sauce, salt, black pepper, and bacon.
3. Divide this filling in the chicken breasts and secure the edges with a toothpick.
4. Brush the remaining BBQ sauce over the chicken breasts.
5. Place the chicken in the crisper plate and spray them with cooking oil.
6. Return the crisper plate to the Ninja Foodi Dual Zone Air Fryer.
7. Choose the Air Fry mode for Zone 1 and set the temperature to 360 degrees F and the time to 20 minutes|
8. Initiate cooking by pressing the START/STOP button.
9. Serve warm.

Chicken Patties And One-dish Chicken Rice

Servings: 8
Cooking Time: 40 Minutes
Ingredients:
- Chicken Patties:
- 450 g chicken thigh mince
- 110 g shredded Mozzarella cheese
- 1 teaspoon dried parsley
- ½ teaspoon garlic powder
- ¼ teaspoon onion powder
- 1 large egg
- 60 g pork rinds, finely ground
- One-Dish Chicken and Rice:
- 190 g long-grain white rice, rinsed and drained
- 120 g cut frozen green beans (do not thaw)
- 1 tablespoon minced fresh ginger
- 3 cloves garlic, minced
- 1 tablespoon toasted sesame oil
- 1 teaspoon kosher salt
- 1 teaspoon black pepper
- 450 g chicken wings, preferably drumettes

Directions:
1. Make the Chicken Patties :
2. In a large bowl, mix chicken mince, Mozzarella, parsley, garlic powder, and onion powder. Form into four patties.
3. Place patties in the freezer for 15 to 20 minutes until they begin to firm up.
4. Whisk egg in a medium bowl. Place the ground pork rinds into a large bowl.
5. Dip each chicken patty into the egg and then press into pork rinds to fully coat. Place patties into the zone 1 air fryer drawer.
6. Adjust the temperature to 180°C and air fry for 12 minutes.
7. Patties will be firm and cooked to an internal temperature of 76°C when done. Serve immediately.
8. Make the One-Dish Chicken and Rice :
9. In a baking pan, combine the rice, green beans, ginger, garlic, sesame oil, salt, and pepper. Stir to combine. Place the chicken wings on top of the rice mixture.
10. Cover the pan with foil. Make a long slash in the foil to allow the pan to vent steam. Place the pan in the zone 2 air fryer drawer. Set the air fryer to 190°C for 30 minutes.
11. Remove the foil. Set the air fryer to 200°C for 10 minutes, or until the wings have browned and rendered fat into the rice and vegetables, turning the wings halfway through the cooking time.

Chicken Shawarma

Servings: 4
Cooking Time: 15 Minutes
Ingredients:
- Shawarma Spice:
- 2 teaspoons dried oregano
- 1 teaspoon ground cinnamon
- 1 teaspoon ground cumin
- 1 teaspoon ground coriander
- 1 teaspoon kosher salt
- ½ teaspoon ground allspice
- ½ teaspoon cayenne pepper
- Chicken:
- 450 g boneless, skinless chicken thighs, cut into large bite-size chunks
- 2 tablespoons vegetable oil
- For Serving:
- Tzatziki
- Pita bread

Directions:
1. For the shawarma spice: In a small bowl, combine the oregano, cayenne, cumin, coriander, salt, cinnamon, and allspice. 2. For the chicken: In a large bowl, toss together the chicken, vegetable oil, and shawarma spice to coat. Marinate at room temperature for 30 minutes or cover and refrigerate for up to 24 hours. 3. Place the chicken in the zone 1 air fryer basket. Set the air fryer to 180°C for 15 minutes, or until the chicken reaches an internal temperature of 75°C. 4. Transfer the chicken to a serving platter. Serve with tzatziki and pita bread.

Curried Orange Honey Chicken

Servings: 4
Cooking Time: 16 To 19 Minutes
Ingredients:
- 340 g boneless, skinless chicken thighs, cut into 1-inch pieces
- 1 yellow bell pepper, cut into 1½-inch pieces
- 1 small red onion, sliced
- Olive oil for misting
- 60 ml chicken stock
- 2 tablespoons honey
- 60 ml orange juice
- 1 tablespoon cornflour
- 2 to 3 teaspoons curry powder

Directions:
1. Preheat the air fryer to 190ºC.
2. Put the chicken thighs, pepper, and red onion in the zone 1 air fryer drawer and mist with olive oil.
3. Roast for 12 to 14 minutes or until the chicken is cooked to 76ºC, shaking the drawer halfway through cooking time.
4. Remove the chicken and vegetables from the air fryer drawer and set aside.
5. In a metal bowl, combine the stock, honey, orange juice, cornflour, and curry powder, and mix well. Add the chicken and vegetables, stir, and put the bowl in the drawer.
6. Return the drawer to the air fryer and roast for 2 minutes. Remove and stir, then roast for 2 to 3 minutes or until the sauce is thickened and bubbly.
7. Serve warm.

Spicy Chicken

Servings: 40
Cooking Time: 35
Ingredients:
- 4 chicken thighs
- 2 cups of butter milk
- 4 chicken legs
- 2 cups of flour
- Salt and black pepper, to taste
- 2 tablespoons garlic powder
- ½ teaspoon onion powder
- 1 teaspoon poultry seasoning
- 1 teaspoon cumin
- 2 tablespoons paprika
- 1 tablespoon olive oil

Directions:
1. Take a bowl and add buttermilk to it.
2. Soak the chicken thighs and chicken legs in the buttermilk for 2 hours.
3. Mix flour, all the seasonings, and olive oil in a small bowl.
4. Take out the chicken pieces from the buttermilk mixture and then dredge them into the flour mixture.
5. Repeat the steps for all the pieces and then arrange them into both the air fryer basket.
6. Set the timer for both the basket by selecting a roast mode for 35-40 minutes at 350 degrees F.
7. Once the cooking cycle complete select the pause button and then take out the basket.
8. Serve and enjoy.

Nutrition:
- (Per serving) Calories 624| Fat17.6 g| Sodium300 mg | Carbs 60g | Fiber 3.5g | Sugar 7.7g | Protein54.2 g

Chicken & Veggies

Servings: 4
Cooking Time: 10 Minutes
Ingredients:
- 450g chicken breast, boneless & cut into pieces
- 2 garlic cloves, minced
- 15ml olive oil
- 239g frozen mix vegetables
- 1 tbsp Italian seasoning
- ½ tsp chilli powder
- ½ tsp garlic powder
- Pepper
- Salt

Directions:
1. In a bowl, toss chicken with remaining ingredients until well coated.
2. Insert a crisper plate in the Ninja Foodi air fryer baskets.
3. Add chicken and vegetables in both baskets.
4. Select zone 1 then select "air fry" mode and set the temperature to 390 degrees F for 10 minutes. Press "match" to match zone 2 settings to zone 1. Press "start/stop" to begin.

Nutrition:
- (Per serving) Calories 221 | Fat 7.6g |Sodium 126mg | Carbs 10.6g | Fiber 3.3g | Sugar 2.7g | Protein 26.3g

Teriyaki Chicken Skewers

Servings: 4
Cooking Time: 16 Minutes
Ingredients:
- 455g boneless chicken thighs, cubed
- 237ml teriyaki marinade
- 16 small wooden skewers
- Sesame seeds for rolling
- Teriyaki Marinade
- ⅓ cup soy sauce
- 59ml chicken broth
- ½ orange, juiced
- 2 tablespoons brown sugar
- 1 teaspoon ginger, grated
- 1 clove garlic, grated

Directions:
1. Blend teriyaki marinade ingredients in a blender.
2. Add chicken and its marinade to a Ziplock bag.
3. Seal this bag, shake it well and refrigerate for 30 minutes.
4. Thread the chicken on the wooden skewers.
5. Place these skewers in the air fryer baskets.
6. Return the air fryer basket 1 to Zone 1, and basket 2 to Zone 2 of the Ninja Foodi 2-Basket Air Fryer.
7. Choose the "Air Fry" mode for Zone 1 at 350 degrees F and 16 minutes of cooking time.
8. Select the "MATCH COOK" option to copy the settings for Zone 2.
9. Initiate cooking by pressing the START/PAUSE BUTTON.
10. Flip the skewers once cooked halfway through.
11. Garnish with sesame seeds.
12. Serve warm.

Nutrition:
- (Per serving) Calories 456 | Fat 16.4g |Sodium 1321mg | Carbs 19.2g | Fiber 2.2g | Sugar 4.2g | Protein 55.2g

Pecan-crusted Chicken Tenders

Servings: 4
Cooking Time: 12 Minutes
Ingredients:
- 2 tablespoons mayonnaise
- 1 teaspoon Dijon mustard
- 455 g boneless, skinless chicken tenders
- ½ teaspoon salt
- ¼ teaspoon ground black pepper
- 75 g chopped roasted pecans, finely ground

Directions:
1. In a small bowl, whisk mayonnaise and mustard until combined. Brush mixture onto chicken tenders on both sides, then sprinkle tenders with salt and pepper.
2. Place pecans in a medium bowl and press each tender into pecans to coat each side.
3. Place tenders into the two ungreased air fryer drawers in a single layer. Adjust the temperature to 190°C and roast for 12 minutes, turning tenders halfway through cooking. Tenders will be golden brown and have an internal temperature of at least 76°C when done. Serve warm.

Cornish Hen

Servings: 4
Cooking Time: 35 Minutes
Ingredients:
- 2 Cornish hens
- 2 tablespoons olive oil
- 2 teaspoons salt
- 1½ teaspoons Italian seasoning
- 1 teaspoon garlic powder
- 1 teaspoon paprika
- ½ teaspoon black pepper
- ½ teaspoon lemon zest

Directions:
1. Mix Italian seasoning with lemon zest, juice, black pepper, paprika, and garlic powder in a bowl.
2. Rub each hen with the seasoning mixture.
3. Tuck the hen wings in and place one in each air fryer basket.
4. Return the air fryer basket 1 to Zone 1, and basket 2 to Zone 2 of the Ninja Foodi 2-Basket Air Fryer.
5. Choose the "Air Fry" mode for Zone 1 and set the temperature to 375 degrees F and 35 minutes of cooking time.
6. Select the "MATCH COOK" option to copy the settings for Zone 2.
7. Initiate cooking by pressing the START/PAUSE BUTTON.
8. Flip the hens once cooked halfway through.
9. Serve warm.

Nutrition:
- (Per serving) Calories 223 | Fat 11.7g |Sodium 721mg | Carbs 13.6g | Fiber 0.7g | Sugar 8g | Protein 15.7g

Spicy Chicken Sandwiches With "fried" Pickles

Servings: 4
Cooking Time: 18 Minutes
Ingredients:
- FOR THE CHICKEN SANDWICHES
- 2 tablespoons all-purpose flour
- 2 large eggs
- 2 teaspoons Louisiana-style hot sauce
- 1 cup panko bread crumbs
- 1 teaspoon paprika
- ½ teaspoon garlic powder
- ¼ teaspoon salt
- ¼ teaspoon freshly ground black pepper
- ¼ teaspoon cayenne pepper (optional)
- 4 thin-sliced chicken cutlets (4 ounces each)
- 2 teaspoons vegetable oil
- 4 hamburger rolls
- FOR THE PICKLES
- 1 cup dill pickle chips, drained
- 1 large egg
- ½ cup panko bread crumbs
- Nonstick cooking spray
- ½ cup ranch dressing, for serving (optional)

Directions:
1. To prep the sandwiches:
2. Set up a breading station with three small shallow bowls. Place the flour in the first bowl. In the second bowl, whisk together the eggs and hot sauce. Combine the panko, paprika, garlic powder, salt, black pepper, and cayenne pepper in the third bowl.
3. Bread the chicken cutlets in this order: First, dip them into the flour, coating both sides. Then, dip into the egg mixture. Finally, coat them in the panko mixture, gently pressing the breading into the chicken to help it adhere. Drizzle the cutlets with the oil.
4. To prep the pickles:
5. Pat the pickles dry with a paper towel.
6. In a small shallow bowl, whisk the egg. Add the panko to a second shallow bowl.
7. Dip the pickles in the egg, then the panko. Mist both sides of the pickles with cooking spray.
8. To cook the chicken and pickles:
9. Install a crisper plate in each of the two baskets. Place the chicken in the Zone 1 basket and insert the basket in the unit. Place the pickles in the Zone 2 basket and insert the basket in the unit.
10. Select Zone 1, select AIR FRY, set the temperature to 390°F, and set the time to 18 minutes.
11. Select Zone 2, select AIR FRY, set the temperature to 400°F, and set the time to 15 minutes. Select SMART FINISH.
12. Press START/PAUSE to begin cooking.
13. When both timers read 10 minutes, press START/PAUSE. Remove the Zone 1 basket and use silicone-tipped tongs to flip the chicken. Reinsert the basket. Remove the Zone 2 basket and shake to redistribute the pickles. Reinsert the basket and press START/PAUSE to resume cooking.
14. When cooking is complete, the breading will be crisp and golden brown and the chicken cooked through . Place one chicken cutlet on each hamburger roll. Serve the "fried" pickles on the side with ranch dressing, if desired.

Chicken Potatoes

Servings: 4
Cooking Time: 22 Minutes
Ingredients:
- 15 ounces canned potatoes drained
- 1 teaspoon olive oil
- 1 teaspoon Lawry's seasoned salt
- ⅛ teaspoons black pepper optional
- 8 ounces boneless chicken breast cubed
- ¼ teaspoon paprika
- ⅜ cup cheddar, shredded
- 4 bacon slices, cooked, cut into strips

Directions:
1. Dice the chicken into small pieces and toss them with olive oil and spices.
2. Drain and dice the potato pieces into smaller cubes.
3. Add potato to the chicken and mix well to coat.
4. Spread the mixture in the two crisper plates in a single layer.
5. Return the crisper plates to the Ninja Foodi Dual Zone Air Fryer.
6. Choose the Air Fry mode for Zone 1 and set the temperature to 390 degrees F and the time to 22 minutes|
7. Select the "MATCH" button to copy the settings for Zone 2.
8. Initiate cooking by pressing the START/STOP button.
9. Top the chicken and potatoes with cheese and bacon.
10. Return the crisper plates to the Ninja Foodi Dual Zone Air Fryer.
11. Select the Max Crisp mode for Zone 1 and set the temperature to 300 degrees F and the time to 5 minutes|
12. Initiate cooking by pressing the START/STOP button.
13. Repeat the same step for Zone 2 to broil the potatoes and chicken in the right drawer.
14. Enjoy with dried herbs on top.

Cracked-pepper Chicken Wings

Servings: 4
Cooking Time: 20 Minutes
Ingredients:
- 450 g chicken wings
- 3 tablespoons vegetable oil
- 60 g all-purpose flour
- ½ teaspoon smoked paprika
- ½ teaspoon garlic powder
- ½ teaspoon kosher salt
- 1½ teaspoons freshly cracked black pepper

Directions:
1. Place the chicken wings in a large bowl. Drizzle the vegetable oil over wings and toss to coat.
2. In a separate bowl, whisk together the flour, paprika, garlic powder, salt, and pepper until combined.
3. Dredge the wings in the flour mixture one at a time, coating them well, and place in the zone 1 air fryer drawer. Set the temperature to 200°C for 20 minutes, turning the wings halfway through the cooking time, until the breading is browned and crunchy.

Vegetables And Sides Recipes

Acorn Squash Slices

Servings: 6
Cooking Time: 10 Minutes
Ingredients:
- 2 medium acorn squashes
- ⅔ cup packed brown sugar
- ½ cup butter, melted

Directions:
1. Cut the squash in half, remove the seeds and slice into ½ inch slices.
2. Place the squash slices in the air fryer baskets.
3. Drizzle brown sugar and butter over the squash slices.
4. Return the air fryer basket 1 to Zone 1, and basket 2 to Zone 2 of the Ninja Foodi 2-Basket Air Fryer.
5. Choose the "Air Fry" mode for Zone 1 and set the temperature to 350 degrees F and 10 minutes of cooking time.
6. Select the "MATCH COOK" option to copy the settings for Zone 2.
7. Initiate cooking by pressing the START/PAUSE BUTTON.
8. Flip the squash once cooked halfway through.
9. Serve.

Nutrition:
- (Per serving) Calories 206 | Fat 3.4g |Sodium 174mg | Carbs 35g | Fiber 9.4g | Sugar 5.9g | Protein 10.6g

Flavourful Mexican Cauliflower

Servings: 4
Cooking Time: 12 Minutes
Ingredients:
- 1 medium cauliflower head, cut into florets
- ½ tsp turmeric
- 1 tsp onion powder
- 2 tsp garlic powder
- 2 tsp parsley
- 1 lime juice
- 30ml olive oil
- 1 tsp chilli powder
- 1 tsp cumin
- Pepper
- Salt

Directions:
1. In a bowl, toss cauliflower florets with onion powder, garlic powder, parsley, oil, chilli powder, turmeric, cumin, pepper, and salt.
2. Insert a crisper plate in the Ninja Foodi air fryer baskets.
3. Add cauliflower florets in both baskets.
4. Select zone 1, then select "air fry" mode and set the temperature to 390 degrees F for 12 minutes. Press "match" to match zone 2 settings to zone 1. Press "start/stop" to begin. Stir halfway through.
5. Drizzle lime juice over cauliflower florets.

Nutrition:
- (Per serving) Calories 108 | Fat 7.4g |Sodium 91mg | Carbs 10g | Fiber 4.1g | Sugar 4.1g | Protein 3.4g

Kale And Spinach Chips

Servings: 2
Cooking Time: 6 Minutes
Ingredients:
- 2 cups spinach, torn in pieces and stem removed
- 2 cups kale, torn in pieces, stems removed
- 1 tablespoon olive oil
- Sea salt, to taste
- ⅓ cup Parmesan cheese

Directions:
1. Take a bowl and add spinach to it.
2. Take another bowl and add kale to it.
3. Season both of them with olive oil and sea salt.
4. Add the kale to the zone 1 basket and spinach to the zone 2 basket.
5. Select AIR FRY mode for zone 1 at 350 degrees F/ 175 degrees C for 6 minutes.
6. Set zone 2 to AIR FRY mode at 350 degrees F/ 175 degrees C for 5 minutes.
7. Once done, take out the crispy chips and sprinkle Parmesan cheese on top. 8. Serve and Enjoy.

Lime Glazed Tofu

Servings: 6
Cooking Time: 14 Minutes
Ingredients:
- ⅔ cup coconut aminos
- 2 (14-oz) packages extra-firm, water-packed tofu, drained
- 6 tablespoons toasted sesame oil
- ⅔ cup lime juice

Directions:
1. Pat dry the tofu bars and slice into half-inch cubes.
2. Toss all the remaining ingredients in a small bowl.
3. Marinate for 4 hours in the refrigerator. Drain off the excess water.
4. Divide the tofu cubes in the two crisper plates.
5. Return the crisper plates to the Ninja Foodi Dual Zone Air Fryer.
6. Choose the Air Fry mode for Zone 1 and set the temperature to 400 degrees F/ 200 degrees C and the time to 14 minutes.
7. Select the "MATCH" button to copy the settings for Zone 2.
8. Initiate cooking by pressing the START/STOP button.
9. Toss the tofu once cooked halfway through, then resume cooking. 10. Serve warm.

Brussels Sprouts

Servings: 2
Cooking Time: 20 Minutes
Ingredients:
- 2 pounds Brussels sprouts
- 2 tablespoons avocado oil
- Salt and pepper, to taste
- 1 cup pine nuts, roasted

Directions:
1. Trim the bottom of the Brussels sprouts.
2. Take a bowl and combine the avocado oil, salt, and black pepper.
3. Toss the Brussels sprouts into the bowl and mix well.
4. Divide the mixture into both air fryer baskets.
5. For zone 1 set to AIR FRY mode for 20 minutes at 390 degrees F/ 200 degrees C.
6. Select the MATCH button for the zone 2 basket.
7. Once the Brussels sprouts get crisp and tender, take out and serve.

Fried Asparagus

Servings: 4
Cooking Time: 6 Minutes
Ingredients:
- ¼ cup mayonnaise
- 4 teaspoons olive oil
- 1½ teaspoons grated lemon zest
- 1 garlic clove, minced
- ½ teaspoon pepper
- ¼ teaspoon seasoned salt
- 1-pound fresh asparagus, trimmed
- 2 tablespoons shredded parmesan cheese
- Lemon wedges (optional)

Directions:
1. In a large bowl, combine the first 6 ingredients.
2. Add the asparagus| toss to coat.
3. Put a crisper plate in both drawers. Put the asparagus in a single layer in each drawer. Top with the parmesan cheese. Place the drawers into the unit.
4. Select zone 1, then AIR FRY, then set the temperature to 375 degrees F/ 190 degrees C with a 6-minute timer. To match zone 2 settings to zone 1, choose MATCH. To begin, select START/STOP.
5. Remove the asparagus from the drawers after the timer has finished.

Caprese Panini With Zucchini Chips

Servings: 4
Cooking Time: 20 Minutes
Ingredients:
- FOR THE PANINI
- 4 tablespoons pesto
- 8 slices Italian-style sandwich bread
- 1 tomato, diced
- 6 ounces fresh mozzarella cheese, shredded
- ¼ cup mayonnaise
- FOR THE ZUCCHINI CHIPS
- ½ cup all-purpose flour
- 2 large eggs
- ¼ teaspoon freshly ground black pepper
- ⅛ teaspoon kosher salt
- ½ cup panko bread crumbs
- ¼ cup grated Parmesan cheese
- 1 teaspoon Italian seasoning
- 1 medium zucchini, cut into ¼-inch-thick rounds
- 2 tablespoons vegetable oil

Directions:
1. To prep the panini: Spread 1 tablespoon of pesto each on 4 slices of the bread. Layer the diced tomato and shredded mozzarella on the other 4 slices of bread. Top the tomato/cheese mixture with the pesto-coated bread, pesto-side down, to form 4 sandwiches.
2. Spread the outside of each sandwich (both bread slices) with a thin layer of the mayonnaise.
3. To prep the zucchini chips: Set up a breading station with three small shallow bowls. Place the flour in the first bowl. In the second bowl, beat together the eggs, salt, and black pepper. Place the panko, Parmesan, and Italian seasoning in the third bowl.
4. Bread the zucchini in this order: First, dip the slices into the flour, coating both sides. Then, dip into the beaten egg. Finally, coat in the panko mixture. Drizzle the zucchini on both sides with the oil.
5. To cook the panini and zucchini chips: Install a crisper plate in each of the two baskets. Place 2 sandwiches in the Zone 1 basket and insert the basket in the unit. Place half of the zucchini chips in a single layer in the Zone 2 basket and insert the basket in the unit.
6. Select Zone 1, select AIR FRY, set the temperature to 375°F, and set the timer to 20 minutes.
7. Select Zone 2, select AIR FRY, set the temperature to 400°F, and set the timer to 20 minutes. Select SMART FINISH.
8. Press START/PAUSE to begin cooking.
9. When the Zone 1 timer reads 15 minutes, press START/PAUSE. Remove the basket, and use silicone-tipped tongs or a spatula to flip the sandwiches. Reinsert the basket and press START/PAUSE to resume cooking.
10. When both timers read 10 minutes, press START/PAUSE. Remove the Zone 1 basket and transfer the sandwiches to a plate. Place the remaining 2 sandwiches into the basket and insert the basket in the unit. Remove the Zone 2 basket and transfer the zucchini chips to a serving plate. Place the remaining zucchini chips in the basket. Reinsert the basket and press START/PAUSE to resume cooking.
11. When the Zone 1 timer reads 5 minutes, press START/PAUSE. Remove the basket and flip the sandwiches. Reinsert the basket and press START/PAUSE to resume cooking.
12. When cooking is complete, the panini should be toasted and the zucchini chips golden brown and crisp.
13. Cut each panini in half. Serve hot with zucchini chips on the side.

Nutrition:
- (Per serving) Calories: 751; Total fat: 39g; Saturated fat: 9.5g; Carbohydrates: 77g; Fiber: 3.5g; Protein: 23g; Sodium: 1,086mg

Healthy Air Fried Veggies

Servings: 4
Cooking Time: 15 Minutes
Ingredients:
- 52g onion, sliced
- 71g broccoli florets
- 116g radishes, sliced
- 15ml olive oil
- 100g Brussels sprouts, cut in half
- 325g cauliflower florets
- 1 tsp balsamic vinegar
- ½ tsp garlic powder
- Pepper
- Salt

Directions:
1. In a bowl, toss veggies with oil, vinegar, garlic powder, pepper, and salt.
2. Insert a crisper plate in the Ninja Foodi air fryer baskets.
3. Add veggies in both baskets.
4. Select zone 1 then select "air fry" mode and set the temperature to 380 degrees F for 15 minutes. Press "match" to match zone 2 settings to zone 1. Press "start/stop" to begin. Stir halfway through.

Nutrition:
- (Per serving) Calories 71 | Fat 3.8g | Sodium 72mg | Carbs 8.8g | Fiber 3.2g | Sugar 3.3g | Protein 2.5g

Falafel

Servings: 6
Cooking Time: 14 Minutes
Ingredients:
- 1 (15.5-oz) can chickpeas, rinsed and drained
- 1 small yellow onion, cut into quarters
- 3 garlic cloves, chopped
- ⅓ cup parsley, chopped
- ⅓ cup cilantro, chopped
- ⅓ cup scallions, chopped
- 1 teaspoon cumin
- ½ teaspoons salt
- ⅛ teaspoons crushed red pepper flakes
- 1 teaspoon baking powder
- 4 tablespoons all-purpose flour
- Olive oil spray

Directions:
1. Dry the chickpeas on paper towels.
2. Add onions and garlic to a food processor and chop them.
3. Add the parsley, salt, cilantro, scallions, cumin, and red pepper flakes.
4. Press the pulse button for 60 seconds, then toss in chickpeas and blend for 3 times until it makes a chunky paste.
5. Stir in baking powder and flour and mix well.
6. Transfer the falafel mixture to a bowl and cover to refrigerate for 3 hours.
7. Make 12 balls out of the falafel mixture.
8. Place 6 falafels in each of the crisper plate and spray them with oil.
9. Return the crisper plate to the Ninja Foodi Dual Zone Air Fryer.
10. Choose the Air Fry mode for Zone 1 and set the temperature to 350 degrees F/ 175 degrees C and the time to 14 minutes.
11. Select the "MATCH" button to copy the settings for Zone 2.
12. Initiate cooking by pressing the START/STOP button.
13. Toss the falafel once cooked halfway through, and resume cooking.
14. Serve warm.

Buffalo Bites

Servings: 6
Cooking Time: 30 Minutes
Ingredients:
- For the bites:
- 1 small cauliflower head, cut into florets
- 2 tablespoons olive oil
- 3 tablespoons buffalo wing sauce
- 3 tablespoons butter, melted
- For the dip:
- 1½ cups 2% cottage cheese
- ¼ cup fat-free plain Greek yogurt
- ¼ cup crumbled blue cheese
- 1 sachet ranch salad dressing mix
- Celery sticks (optional)

Directions:
1. In a large bowl, combine the cauliflower and oil| toss to coat.
2. Place a crisper plate in each drawer. Put the coated cauliflower florets in each drawer in a single layer. Place the drawers in the unit.
3. Select zone 1, then AIR FRY, then set the temperature to 360 degrees F/ 180 degrees C with a 15-minute timer. To match zone 2 settings to zone 1, choose MATCH. To begin, select START/STOP.
4. Remove the cauliflower from the drawers after the timer has finished.
5. Combine the buffalo sauce and melted butter in a large mixing bowl. Put in the cauliflower and toss to coat. Place on a serving dish and serve.
6. Combine the dip ingredients in a small bowl. Serve with the cauliflower and celery sticks, if desired.

Green Beans With Baked Potatoes

Servings: 2
Cooking Time: 45 Minutes
Ingredients:
- 2 cups green beans
- 2 large potatoes, cubed
- 3 tablespoons olive oil
- 1 teaspoon seasoned salt
- ½ teaspoon chili powder
- ⅙ teaspoon garlic powder
- ¼ teaspoon onion powder

Directions:
1. Take a large bowl and pour olive oil into it.
2. Add all the seasoning in the olive oil and whisk it well.
3. Toss the green beans in and mix well and then transfer to zone 1 basket of the air fryer.
4. Season the potatoes with the oil seasoning and add them to the zone 2 basket.
5. Press the Sync button.
6. Once the cooking cycle is complete, take out and serve.

Pepper Poppers

Servings: 24
Cooking Time: 20 Minutes
Ingredients:
- 8 ounces cream cheese, softened
- ¾ cup shredded cheddar cheese
- ¾ cup shredded Monterey Jack cheese
- 6 bacon strips, cooked and crumbled
- ¼ teaspoon salt
- ¼ teaspoon garlic powder
- ¼ teaspoon chili powder
- ¼ teaspoon smoked paprika
- 1-pound fresh jalapeño peppers, halved lengthwise and deseeded
- ½ cup dry breadcrumbs
- Sour cream, French onion dip, or ranch salad dressing (optional)

Directions:
1. In a large bowl, combine the cheeses, bacon, and seasonings| mix well. Spoon 1½ to 2 tablespoons of the mixture into each pepper half. Roll them in the breadcrumbs.
2. Place a crisper plate in each drawer. Put the prepared peppers in a single layer in each drawer. Insert the drawers into the unit.
3. Select zone 1, then AIR FRY, then set the temperature to 360 degrees F/ 180 degrees C with a 20-minute timer. To match zone 2 settings to zone 1, choose MATCH. To begin, select START/STOP.
4. Remove the peppers from the drawers after the timer has finished.

Fried Olives

Servings: 6
Cooking Time: 9 Minutes
Ingredients:
- 2 cups blue cheese stuffed olives, drained
- ½ cup all-purpose flour
- 1 cup panko breadcrumbs
- ½ teaspoon garlic powder
- 1 pinch oregano
- 2 eggs

Directions:
1. Mix flour with oregano and garlic powder in a bowl and beat two eggs in another bowl.
2. Spread panko breadcrumbs in a bowl.
3. Coat all the olives with the flour mixture, dip in the eggs and then coat with the panko breadcrumbs.
4. As you coat the olives, place them in the two crisper plates in a single layer, then spray them with cooking oil.
5. Return the crisper plates to the Ninja Foodi Dual Zone Air Fryer.
6. Choose the Air Fry mode for Zone 1 and set the temperature to 375 degrees F/ 190 degrees C and the time to 9 minutes.
7. Select the "MATCH" button to copy the settings for Zone 2.
8. Initiate cooking by pressing the START/STOP button.
9. Flip the olives once cooked halfway through, then resume cooking.
10. Serve.

Breaded Summer Squash

Servings: 4
Cooking Time: 10 Minutes
Ingredients:
- 4 cups yellow summer squash, sliced
- 3 tablespoons olive oil
- ½ teaspoon salt
- ½ teaspoon pepper
- ⅛ teaspoon cayenne pepper
- ¾ cup panko bread crumbs
- ¾ cup grated Parmesan cheese

Directions:
1. Mix crumbs, cheese, cayenne pepper, black pepper, salt and oil in a bowl.
2. Coat the squash slices with the breadcrumb mixture.
3. Place these slices in the air fryer baskets.
4. Return the air fryer basket 1 to Zone 1, and basket 2 to Zone 2 of the Ninja Foodi 2-Basket Air Fryer.
5. Choose the "Air Fry" mode for Zone 1 at 350 degrees F and 10 minutes of cooking time.
6. Select the "MATCH COOK" option to copy the settings for Zone 2.
7. Initiate cooking by pressing the START/PAUSE BUTTON.
8. Flip the squash slices once cooked half way through.
9. Serve warm.

Nutrition:
- (Per serving) Calories 193 | Fat 1g |Sodium 395mg | Carbs 38.7g | Fiber 1.6g | Sugar 0.9g | Protein 6.6g

Air-fried Tofu Cutlets With Cacio E Pepe Brussels Sprouts

Servings: 4
Cooking Time: 25 Minutes
Ingredients:
- FOR THE TOFU CUTLETS
- 1 (14-ounce) package extra-firm tofu, drained
- 1 cup panko bread crumbs
- ¼ cup grated pecorino romano or Parmesan cheese
- 1 teaspoon garlic powder
- 1 teaspoon onion powder
- ¼ teaspoon kosher salt
- 1 tablespoon vegetable oil
- 4 lemon wedges, for serving
- FOR THE BRUSSELS SPROUTS
- 1 pound Brussels sprouts, trimmed
- 1 tablespoon vegetable oil
- 2 tablespoons grated pecorino romano or Parmesan cheese
- ½ teaspoon freshly ground black pepper, plus more to taste
- ¼ teaspoon kosher salt

Directions:
1. To prep the tofu: Cut the tofu horizontally into 4 slabs.
2. In a shallow bowl, mix together the panko, cheese, garlic powder, onion powder, and salt. Press both sides of each tofu slab into the panko mixture. Drizzle both sides with the oil.
3. To prep the Brussels sprouts: Cut the Brussels sprouts in half through the root end.
4. In a large bowl, combine the Brussels sprouts and olive oil. Mix to coat.
5. To cook the tofu cutlets and Brussels sprouts: Install a crisper plate in each of the two baskets. Place the tofu cutlets in a single layer in the Zone 1 basket and insert the basket in the unit. Place the Brussels sprouts in the Zone 2 basket and insert the basket in the unit.
6. Select Zone 1, select AIR FRY, set the temperature to 400°F, and set the timer to 20 minutes.
7. Select Zone 2, select ROAST, set the temperature to 400°F, and set the timer to 25 minutes. Select SMART FINISH.
8. Press START/PAUSE to begin cooking.
9. When both timers read 5 minutes, press START/PAUSE. Remove the Zone 1 basket and use a pair of silicone-tipped tongs to flip the tofu cutlets, then reinsert the basket in the unit. Remove the Zone 2 basket and sprinkle the cheese and black pepper over the Brussels sprouts. Reinsert the basket and press START/PAUSE to resume cooking.
10. When cooking is complete, the tofu should be crisp and the Brussels sprouts tender and beginning to brown.
11. Squeeze the lemon wedges over the tofu cutlets. Stir the Brussels sprouts, then season with the salt and additional black pepper to taste.

Nutrition:
- (Per serving) Calories: 319; Total fat: 15g; Saturated fat: 3.5g; Carbohydrates: 27g; Fiber: 6g; Protein: 20g; Sodium: 402mg

Sweet Potatoes & Brussels Sprouts

Servings: 8
Cooking Time: 35 Minutes
Ingredients:
- 340g sweet potatoes, cubed
- 30ml olive oil
- 150g onion, cut into pieces
- 352g Brussels sprouts, halved
- Pepper
- Salt
- For glaze:
- 78ml ketchup
- 115ml balsamic vinegar
- 15g mustard
- 29 ml honey

Directions:
1. In a bowl, toss Brussels sprouts, oil, onion, sweet potatoes, pepper, and salt.
2. Insert a crisper plate in the Ninja Foodi air fryer baskets.
3. Add Brussels sprouts and sweet potato mixture in both baskets.
4. Select zone 1, then select "air fry" mode and set the temperature to 390 degrees F for 25 minutes. Press "match" to match zone 2 settings to zone 1. Press "start/stop" to begin. Stir halfway through.
5. Meanwhile, add vinegar, ketchup, honey, and mustard to a saucepan and cook over medium heat for 5-10 minutes.
6. Toss cooked sweet potatoes and Brussels sprouts with sauce.

Nutrition:
- (Per serving) Calories 142 | Fat 4.2g | Sodium 147mg | Carbs 25.2g | Fiber 4g | Sugar 8.8g | Protein 2.9g

Chickpea Fritters

Servings: 6
Cooking Time: 6 Minutes
Ingredients:
- 237ml plain yogurt
- 2 tablespoons sugar
- 1 tablespoon honey
- ½ teaspoon salt
- ½ teaspoon black pepper
- ½ teaspoon crushed red pepper flakes
- 1 can (28g) chickpeas, drained
- 1 teaspoon ground cumin
- ½ teaspoon salt
- ½ teaspoon garlic powder
- ½ teaspoon ground ginger
- 1 large egg
- ½ teaspoon baking soda
- ½ cup fresh coriander, chopped
- 2 green onions, sliced

Directions:
1. Mash chickpeas with rest of the ingredients in a food processor.
2. Layer the two air fryer baskets with a parchment paper.
3. Drop the batter in the baskets spoon by spoon.
4. Return the air fryer basket 1 to Zone 1, and basket 2 to Zone 2 of the Ninja Foodi 2-Basket Air Fryer.
5. Choose the "Air Fry" mode for Zone 1 at 400 degrees F and 6 minutes of cooking time.
6. Select the "MATCH COOK" option to copy the settings for Zone 2.
7. Initiate cooking by pressing the START/PAUSE BUTTON.
8. Flip the fritters once cooked halfway through.
9. Serve warm.

Nutrition:
- (Per serving) Calories 284 | Fat 7.9g |Sodium 704mg | Carbs 38.1g | Fiber 1.9g | Sugar 1.9g | Protein 14.8g

Potato And Parsnip Latkes With Baked Apples

Servings: 4
Cooking Time: 20 Minutes
Ingredients:
- FOR THE LATKES
- 2 medium russet potatoes, peeled
- 1 large egg white
- 2 tablespoons all-purpose flour
- ¼ teaspoon garlic powder
- ¼ teaspoon kosher salt
- ¼ teaspoon freshly ground black pepper
- 1 medium parsnip, peeled and shredded
- 2 scallions, thinly sliced
- 2 tablespoons vegetable oil
- FOR THE BAKED APPLES
- 2 Golden Delicious apples, peeled and diced
- 2 tablespoons granulated sugar
- 2 teaspoons unsalted butter, cut into small pieces

Directions:
1. To prep the latkes: Grate the potatoes using the large holes of a box grater. Squeeze as much liquid out of the potatoes as you can into a large bowl. Set the potatoes aside in a separate bowl.
2. Let the potato liquid sit for 5 minutes, during which time the potato starch will settle to the bottom of the bowl. Pour off the water that has risen to the top, leaving the potato starch in the bowl.
3. Add the egg white, flour, salt, and black pepper to the potato starch to form a thick paste. Add the potatoes, parsnip, and scallions and mix well. Divide the mixture into 4 patties. Brush both sides of each patty with the oil.
4. To prep the baked apples: Place the apples in the Zone 2 basket. Sprinkle the sugar and butter over the top.
5. To cook the latkes and apples: Install a crisper plate in the Zone 1 basket. Place the latkes in the basket in a single layer, then insert the basket in the unit. Insert the Zone 2 basket in the unit.
6. Select Zone 1, select AIR FRY, set the temperature to 375°F, and set the timer to 15 minutes.
7. Select Zone 2, select BAKE, set the temperature to 330°F, and set the timer to 20 minutes. Select SMART FINISH.
8. Press START/PAUSE to begin cooking.
9. When both timers read 5 minutes, press START/PAUSE. Remove the Zone 1 basket and use silicone-tipped tongs or a spatula to flip the latkes. Reinsert the basket in the unit. Remove the Zone 2 basket and gently mash the apples with a fork or the back of a spoon. Reinsert the basket and press START/PAUSE to resume cooking.
10. When cooking is complete, the latkes should be golden brown and cooked through and the apples very soft.
11. Transfer the latkes to a plate and serve with apples on the side.

Nutrition:
- (Per serving) Calories: 257; Total fat: 9g; Saturated fat: 2g; Carbohydrates: 42g; Fiber: 5.5g; Protein: 4g; Sodium: 91mg

Bbq Corn

Servings: 4
Cooking Time: 10 Minutes
Ingredients:
- 450g can baby corn, drained & rinsed
- 56g BBQ sauce
- ½ tsp Sriracha sauce

Directions:
1. In a bowl, toss the baby corn with sriracha sauce and BBQ sauce until well coated.
2. Insert a crisper plate in the Ninja Foodi air fryer baskets.
3. Add the baby corn to both baskets.
4. Select zone 1, then select "air fry" mode and set the temperature to 390 degrees F for 10 minutes. Press "match" to match zone 2 settings to zone 1. Press "start/stop" to begin. Stir halfway through.

Nutrition:
- (Per serving) Calories 46 | Fat 0.1g |Sodium 446mg | Carbs 10.2g | Fiber 2.8g | Sugar 5.9g | Protein 0.9g

Desserts Recipes

Sweet Potato Donut Holes

Servings: 18 Donut Holes
Cooking Time: 4 To 5 Minutes
Ingredients:
- 125 g plain flour
- 65 g granulated sugar
- ¼ teaspoon baking soda
- 1 teaspoon baking powder
- ⅛ teaspoon salt
- 125 g cooked & mashed purple sweet potatoes
- 1 egg, beaten
- 2 tablespoons butter, melted
- 1 teaspoon pure vanilla extract
- Coconut, or avocado oil for misting or cooking spray

Directions:
1. Preheat the air fryer to 200°C.
2. In a large bowl, stir together the flour, sugar, baking soda, baking powder, and salt.
3. In a separate bowl, combine the potatoes, egg, butter, and vanilla and mix well.
4. Add potato mixture to dry ingredients and stir into a soft dough.
5. Shape dough into 1½-inch balls. Mist lightly with oil or cooking spray.
6. Place the donut holes in the two air fryer baskets, leaving a little space in between. Cook for 4 to 5 minutes, until done in center and lightly browned outside.

Fruity Blackberry Crisp

Servings: 4
Cooking Time: 15 Minutes
Ingredients:
- 2 cups blackberries
- ⅓ cup powdered erythritol
- 2 tablespoons lemon juice
- ¼ teaspoon xanthan gum
- 1 cup Crunchy Granola

Directions:
1. Mix erythritol, blackberries, xanthan gum, and lemon juice in a large bowl.
2. Place into 6&quot| round baking dish and cover with a sheet of foil. Put into the air fryer basket.
3. Set the temperature to 350°F, then set the timer for 12 minutes.
4. When the goes off, remove the foil and shake well.
5. Sprinkle granola on the top of mixture and place back to the air fryer basket.
6. Set the temperature to 320°F, then set the timer for 3 minutes or until the top is golden brown.
7. Serve immediately.

Pumpkin Hand Pies Blueberry Hand Pies

Servings: 4
Cooking Time: 15 Minutes
Ingredients:
- FOR THE PUMPKIN HAND PIES
- ½ cup pumpkin pie filling (from a 15-ounce can)
- ⅓ cup half-and-half
- 1 large egg
- ½ refrigerated pie crust (from a 14.1-ounce package)
- 1 large egg yolk
- 1 tablespoon whole milk
- FOR THE BLUEBERRY HAND PIES
- ¼ cup blueberries
- 2 tablespoons granulated sugar
- 1 tablespoon grated lemon zest (optional)
- ¼ teaspoon cornstarch
- 1 teaspoon fresh lemon juice
- ⅛ teaspoon kosher salt
- ½ refrigerated pie crust (from a 14.1-ounce package)
- 1 large egg yolk
- 1 tablespoon whole milk
- ½ teaspoon turbinado sugar

Directions:
1. To prep the pumpkin hand pies: In a small bowl, mix the pumpkin pie filling, half-and-half, and whole egg until well combined and smooth.
2. Cut the dough in half to form two wedges. Divide the pumpkin pie filling between the wedges. Fold the crust over to completely encase the filling. Using a fork, crimp the edges, forming a tight seal.
3. In a small bowl, whisk together the egg yolk and milk. Brush over the pastry. Carefully cut two small vents in the top of each pie.
4. To prep the blueberry hand pies: In a small bowl, combine the blueberries, granulated sugar, lemon zest (if using), cornstarch, lemon juice, and salt.
5. Cut the dough in half to form two wedges. Divide the blueberry filling between the wedges. Fold the crust over to completely encase the filling. Using a fork, crimp the edges, forming a tight seal.
6. In a small bowl, whisk together the egg yolk and milk. Brush over the pastry. Sprinkle with the turbinado sugar. Carefully cut two small vents in the top of each pie.
7. To cook the hand pies: Install a crisper plate in each of the two baskets. Place the pumpkin hand pies in the Zone 1 basket and insert the basket in the unit. Place the blueberry hand pies in the Zone 2 basket and insert the basket in the unit.
8. Select Zone 1, select AIR FRY, set the temperature to 350°F, and set the timer to 15 minutes. Select MATCH COOK to match Zone 2 settings to Zone 1.
9. Press START/PAUSE to begin cooking.
10. When cooking is complete, the pie crust should be crisp and golden brown and the filling bubbling.
11. Let the hand pies cool for at least 30 minutes before serving.

Nutrition:
- (Per serving) Calories: 588; Total fat: 33g; Saturated fat: 14g; Carbohydrates: 68g; Fiber: 0.5g; Protein: 10g; Sodium: 583mg

Citrus Mousse

Servings: 4
Cooking Time: 12 Minutes
Ingredients:
- 8 ounces cream cheese, softened
- 1 cup heavy cream
- 4 tablespoons fresh lime juice
- 4 tablespoons maple syrup
- Pinch of salt

Directions:
1. For mousse: Press "Zone 1" and "Zone 2" and then rotate the knob for each zone to select "Bake".
2. Set the temperature to 350 degrees F/ 175 degrees C for both zones and then set the time for 5 minutes to preheat.
3. In a bowl, add all the ingredients and mix until well combined.
4. Transfer the mixture into 4 ramekins.
5. After preheating, arrange 2 ramekins into the basket of each zone.
6. Slide each basket into Air Fryer and set the time for 12 minutes.
7. After cooking time is completed, remove the ramekins from Air Fryer.
8. Set the ramekins aside to cool.
9. Refrigerate the ramekins for at least 3 hours before serving.

Sweet Protein Powder Doughnut Holes

Servings: 6 (2 Per Serving)
Cooking Time: 6 Minutes
Ingredients:
- ½ cup blanched finely ground almond flour
- ½ cup low-carb vanilla protein powder
- ½ cup granular erythritol
- ½ teaspoon baking powder
- 1 large egg
- 5 tablespoons unsalted butter, melted
- ½ teaspoon vanilla extract

Directions:
1. Stir all ingredients well in a large bowl. Put into the freezer for at least 20 minutes.
2. Wet your hands with water, then form the dough into 12 balls with your hands.
3. Slice a sheet of parchment which fit your air fryer basket. Handling in batches if needed, put doughnut holes into the air fryer basket onto the parchment.
4. Set the temperature to 380°F, then set the timer for 6 minutes.
5. Turn doughnut holes over halfway through the cooking time.
6. Allow them to cool fully before serving.

Zesty Cranberry Scones

Servings: 8
Cooking Time: 16 Minutes.
Ingredients:
- 4 cups of flour
- ½ cup brown sugar
- 2 tablespoons baking powder
- ½ teaspoon ground nutmeg
- ½ teaspoon salt
- ½ cup butter, chilled and diced
- 2 cups fresh cranberry
- ⅔ cup sugar
- 2 tablespoons orange zest
- 1 ¼ cups half and half cream
- 2 eggs

Directions:
1. Whisk flour with baking powder, salt, nutmeg, and both the sugars in a bowl.
2. Stir in egg and cream, mix well to form a smooth dough.
3. Fold in cranberries along with the orange zest.
4. Knead this dough well on a work surface.
5. Cut 3-inch circles out of the dough.
6. Divide the scones in the crisper plates and spray them with cooking oil.
7. Return the crisper plates to the Ninja Foodi Dual Zone Air Fryer.
8. Choose the Air Fry mode for Zone 1 and set the temperature to 375 degrees F and the time to 16 minutes.
9. Select the "MATCH" button to copy the settings for Zone 2.
10. Initiate cooking by pressing the START/STOP button.
11. Flip the scones once cooked halfway and resume cooking.
12. Enjoy!

Nutrition:
- (Per serving) Calories 204 | Fat 9g | Sodium 91mg | Carbs 27g | Fiber 2.4g | Sugar 15g | Protein 1.3g

Pineapple Wontons

Servings: 5
Cooking Time: 15 To 18 Minutes
Ingredients:
- 225 g cream cheese
- 170 g finely chopped fresh pineapple
- 20 wonton wrappers
- Cooking oil spray

Directions:
1. In a small microwave-safe bowl, heat the cream cheese in the microwave on high power for 20 seconds to soften.
2. In a medium bowl, stir together the cream cheese and pineapple until mixed well.
3. Lay out the wonton wrappers on a work surface. A clean table or large cutting board works well.
4. Spoon 1½ teaspoons of the cream cheese mixture onto each wrapper. Be careful not to overfill.
5. Fold each wrapper diagonally across to form a triangle. Bring the 2 bottom corners up toward each other. Do not close the wrapper yet. Bring up the 2 open sides and push out any air. Squeeze the open edges together to seal.
6. Preheat the air fryer to 200°C.
7. Place the wontons into the two drawers. Spray the wontons with the cooking oil.
8. Cook wontons for 10 minutes, then remove the drawers, flip each wonton, and spray them with more oil. Reinsert the drawers to resume cooking for 5 to 8 minutes more until the wontons are light golden brown and crisp.
9. When the cooking is complete, cool for 5 minutes before serving.

Victoria Sponge Cake

Servings: 8
Cooking Time: 16 Minutes
Ingredients:
- Sponge Cake Ingredients
- 400g self-rising flour
- 450g caster sugar
- 50g lemon curd
- 200g butter
- 4 medium eggs
- 1 tablespoon vanilla essence
- 480ml skimmed milk
- 1 tablespoon olive oil
- 4 tablespoons strawberry jam
- Strawberry buttercream
- 115g butter
- 210g icing sugar
- ½ teaspoon strawberry food coloring
- 1 tablespoon single cream
- 1 teaspoon vanilla essence
- 1 teaspoon maple syrup

Directions:
1. Mix sugar and butter in a bowl using a hand mixer.
2. Beat eggs with oil, and vanilla in a bowl with the mixer until creamy.
3. Stir in milk, flour and curd then mix well.
4. Add butter mixture then mix well.
5. Divide this mixture in two 4 inches greased cake pans.
6. Place one pan in each air fryer basket.
7. Return the air fryer basket 1 to Zone 1, and basket 2 to Zone 2 of the Ninja Foodi 2-Basket Air Fryer.
8. Choose the "Air Fry" mode for Zone 1 and set the temperature to 375 degrees F and 16 minutes of cooking time.
9. Select the "MATCH COOK" option to copy the settings for Zone 2.
10. Initiate cooking by pressing the START/PAUSE BUTTON.
11. Meanwhile, blend the buttercream ingredients in a mixer until fluffy.
12. Place one cake on a plate and top it with the buttercream.
13. Top it jam and then with the other cake.
14. Serve.

Nutrition:
- (Per serving) Calories 284 | Fat 16g |Sodium 252mg | Carbs 31.6g | Fiber 0.9g | Sugar 6.6g | Protein 3.7g

Moist Chocolate Espresso Muffins

Servings: 8
Cooking Time: 18 Minutes
Ingredients:
- 1 egg
- 177ml milk
- ½ tsp baking soda
- ½ tsp espresso powder
- ½ tsp baking powder
- 50g cocoa powder
- 78ml vegetable oil
- 1 tsp apple cider vinegar
- 1 tsp vanilla
- 150g brown sugar
- 150g all-purpose flour
- ½ tsp salt

Directions:
1. In a bowl, whisk egg, vinegar, oil, brown sugar, vanilla, and milk.
2. Add flour, cocoa powder, baking soda, baking powder, espresso powder, and salt and stir until well combined.
3. Pour batter into the silicone muffin moulds.
4. Insert a crisper plate in Ninja Foodi air fryer baskets.
5. Place muffin moulds in both baskets.
6. Select zone 1 then select "bake" mode and set the temperature to 320 degrees F for 18 minutes. Press match cook to match zone 2 settings to zone 1. Press "start/stop" to begin.

Nutrition:
- (Per serving) Calories 222 | Fat 11g |Sodium 251mg | Carbs 29.6g | Fiber 2g | Sugar 14.5g | Protein 4g

Monkey Bread

Servings: 12
Cooking Time: 10 Minutes
Ingredients:
- Bread
- 12 Rhodes white dinner rolls
- ½ cup brown sugar
- 1 teaspoon cinnamon
- 4 tablespoons butter melted
- Glaze
- ½ cup powdered sugar
- 1-2 tablespoons milk
- ½ teaspoon vanilla

Directions:
1. Mix brown sugar, cinnamon and butter in a bowl.
2. Cut the dinner rolls in half and dip them in the sugar mixture.
3. Place these buns in a greased baking pan and pour the remaining butter on top.
4. Place the buns in the air fryer baskets.
5. Return the air fryer basket 1 to Zone 1, and basket 2 to Zone 2 of the Ninja Foodi 2-Basket Air Fryer.
6. Choose the "Air Fry" mode for Zone 1 at 350 degrees F and 10 minutes of cooking time.
7. Initiate cooking by pressing the START/PAUSE BUTTON.
8. Flip the rolls once cooked halfway through.
9. Meanwhile, mix milk, vanilla and sugar in a bowl.
10. Pour the glaze over the air fried rolls.
11. Serve.

Nutrition:
- (Per serving) Calories 192 | Fat 9.3g |Sodium 133mg | Carbs 27.1g | Fiber 1.4g | Sugar 19g | Protein 3.2g

Gluten-free Spice Cookies

Servings: 4
Cooking Time: 12 Minutes
Ingredients:
- 4 tablespoons unsalted butter, at room temperature
- 2 tablespoons agave nectar
- 1 large egg
- 2 tablespoons water
- 240 g almond flour
- 100 g granulated sugar
- 2 teaspoons ground ginger
- 1 teaspoon ground cinnamon
- ½ teaspoon freshly grated nutmeg
- 1 teaspoon baking soda
- ¼ teaspoon kosher, or coarse sea salt

Directions:
1. Line the bottom of the air fryer basket with baking paper cut to fit.
2. In a large bowl, using a hand mixer, beat together the butter, agave, egg, and water on medium speed until light and fluffy.
3. Add the almond flour, sugar, ginger, cinnamon, nutmeg, baking soda, and salt. Beat on low speed until well combined.
4. Roll the dough into 2-tablespoon balls and arrange them on the baking paper in the basket. Set the air fryer to 165°C, and cook for 12 minutes, or until the tops of cookies are lightly browned.
5. Transfer to a wire rack and let cool completely. Store in an airtight container for up to a week.

Chocolate Chip Cake

Servings: 4
Cooking Time: 15 Minutes
Ingredients:
- Salt, pinch
- 2 eggs, whisked
- ½ cup brown sugar
- ½ cup butter, melted
- 10 tablespoons almond milk
- ¼ teaspoon vanilla extract
- ½ teaspoon baking powder
- 1 cup all-purpose flour
- 1 cup chocolate chips
- ½ cup cocoa powder

Directions:
1. Take 2 round baking pans that fit inside the baskets of the air fryer and line them with baking paper.
2. In a bowl with an electric beater, mix the eggs, brown sugar, butter, almond milk, and vanilla extract.
3. In a second bowl, mix the flour, cocoa powder, baking powder, and salt.
4. Slowly add the dry to the wet Ingredients:.
5. Fold in the chocolate chips and mix well with a spoon or spatula.
6. Divide this batter into the round baking pans.
7. Set the time for zone 1 to 16 minutes at 350 degrees F on AIR FRY mode.
8. Select the MATCH button for the zone 2 basket.
9. After the time is up, check. If they're not done, let them AIR FRY for one more minute.
10. Once it is done, serve.

Churros

Servings: 8
Cooking Time: 10 Minutes
Ingredients:
- 1 cup water
- 1/3 cup unsalted butter, cut into cubes
- 2 tablespoons granulated sugar
- 1/4 teaspoon salt
- 1 cup all-purpose flour
- 2 large eggs
- 1 teaspoon vanilla extract
- Cooking oil spray
- For the cinnamon-sugar coating:
- 1/2 cup granulated sugar
- 3/4 teaspoon ground cinnamon

Directions:
1. Add the water, butter, sugar, and salt to a medium pot. Bring to a boil over medium-high heat.
2. Reduce the heat to medium-low and stir in the flour. Cook, stirring constantly with a rubber spatula until the dough is smooth and comes together.
3. Remove the dough from the heat and place it in a mixing bowl. Allow 4 minutes for cooling.
4. In a mixing bowl, beat the eggs and vanilla extract with an electric hand mixer or stand mixer until the dough comes together. The finished product will resemble gluey mashed potatoes. Press the lumps together into a ball with your hands, then transfer to a large piping bag with a large star-shaped tip. Pipe out the churros.
5. Install a crisper plate in both drawers. Place half the churros in the zone 1 drawer and half in zone 2's, then insert the drawers into the unit.
6. Select zone 1, select AIR FRY, set temperature to 390°F, and set time to 12 minutes. Select MATCH to match zone 2 settings to zone 1. Press the START/STOP button to begin cooking.
7. In a shallow bowl, combine the granulated sugar and cinnamon.
8. Immediately transfer the baked churros to the bowl with the sugar mixture and toss to coat.

Speedy Chocolate Espresso Mini Cheesecake

Servings: 2
Cooking Time: 15 Minutes
Ingredients:
- 1/2 cup walnuts
- 2 tablespoons salted butter
- 2 tablespoons granular erythritol
- 4 ounces full-fat cream cheese, softened
- 1 large egg
- 1/2 teaspoon vanilla extract
- 2 tablespoons powdered erythritol
- 2 teaspoons unsweetened cocoa powder
- 1 teaspoon espresso powder

Directions:
1. Put butter, granular erythritol and walnuts in a food processor. Pulse until all the ingredients stick together to form a dough.
2. Place dough into 4"| springform pan and put into the air fryer basket.
3. Set the temperature to 400°F, then set the timer for 5 minutes.
4. When timer goes off, remove crust and allow it to cool.
5. Combine cream cheese with vanilla extract, egg, powdered erythritol, espresso powder and cocoa powder until smooth in a medium bowl.
6. Pour mixture on top of baked walnut crust and put into the air fryer basket.
7. Set the temperature for 300°F, then set the timer for 10 minutes.
8. Once fully cooked, allow to chill for 2 hours before serving.

Caramelized Fruit Skewers

Servings: 4
Cooking Time: 3 To 5 Minutes
Ingredients:
- 2 peaches, peeled, pitted, and thickly sliced
- 3 plums, halved and pitted
- 3 nectarines, halved and pitted
- 1 tablespoon honey
- 1/2 teaspoon ground cinnamon
- 1/4 teaspoon ground allspice
- Pinch cayenne pepper
- Special Equipment:
- 8 metal skewers

Directions:
1. Preheat the air fryer to 204°C.
2. Thread, alternating peaches, plums, and nectarines, onto the metal skewers that fit into the air fryer.
3. Thoroughly combine the honey, cinnamon, allspice, and cayenne in a small bowl. Brush the glaze generously over the fruit skewers.
4. Transfer the fruit skewers to the two air fryer drawers.
5. Air fry for 3 to 5 minutes, or until the fruit is caramelized.
6. Remove from the drawers.
7. Let the fruit skewers rest for 5 minutes before serving.

Walnuts Fritters

Servings: 6
Cooking Time: 15 Minutes.
Ingredients:
- 1 cup all-purpose flour
- ½ cup walnuts, chopped
- ¼ cup white sugar
- ¼ cup milk
- 1 egg
- 1 ½ teaspoons baking powder
- 1 pinch salt
- Cooking spray
- 2 tablespoons white sugar
- ½ teaspoon ground cinnamon
- Glaze:
- ½ cup confectioners' sugar
- 1 tablespoon milk
- ½ teaspoon caramel extract
- ¼ teaspoons ground cinnamon

Directions:
1. Layer both crisper plate with parchment paper.
2. Grease the parchment paper with cooking spray.
3. Whisk flour with milk, ¼ cup of sugar, egg, baking powder, and salt in a small bowl.
4. Separately mix 2 tablespoons of sugar with cinnamon in another bowl, toss in walnuts and mix well to coat.
5. Stir in flour mixture and mix until combined.
6. Drop the fritters mixture using a cookie scoop into the two crisper plate.
7. Return the crisper plate to the Ninja Foodi Dual Zone Air Fryer.
8. Choose the Air Fry mode for Zone 1 and set the temperature to 375 degrees F and the time to 15 minutes.
9. Select the "MATCH" button to copy the settings for Zone 2.
10. Initiate cooking by pressing the START/STOP button.
11. Flip the fritters once cooked halfway through, then resume cooking.
12. Meanwhile, whisk milk, caramel extract, confectioners' sugar, and cinnamon in a bowl.
13. Transfer fritters to a wire rack and allow them to cool.
14. Drizzle with a glaze over the fritters.

Nutrition:
- (Per serving) Calories 391 | Fat 24g | Sodium 142mg | Carbs 38.5g | Fiber 3.5g | Sugar 21g | Protein 6.6g

Maple-pecan Tart With Sea Salt

Servings: 8
Cooking Time: 25 Minutes
Ingredients:
- Tart Crust:
- Vegetable oil spray
- 75 g unsalted butter, softened
- 50 g firmly packed brown sugar
- 125 g plain flour
- ¼ teaspoon kosher, or coarse sea salt
- Filling:
- 4 tablespoons unsalted butter, diced
- 95 g packed brown sugar
- 60 ml pure maple syrup
- 60 ml whole milk
- ¼ teaspoon pure vanilla extract
- 190 g finely chopped pecans
- ¼ teaspoon flaked sea salt

Directions:
1. For the crust: Line a baking pan with foil, leaving a couple of inches of overhang. Spray the foil with vegetable oil spray. 2. In a medium bowl, combine the butter and brown sugar. Beat with an electric mixer on medium-low speed until light and fluffy. Add the flour and kosher salt and beat until the ingredients are well blended. Transfer the mixture to the prepared pan. Press it evenly into the bottom of the pan. 3. Place the pan in the zone 1 air fryer drawer. Set the temperature to 176°C and cook for 13 minutes. When the crust has 5 minutes left to cook, start the filling. 4. For the filling: In a medium saucepan, combine the butter, brown sugar, maple syrup, and milk. Bring to a simmer, stirring occasionally. When it begins simmering, cook for 1 minute. Remove from the heat and stir in the vanilla and pecans. 5. Carefully pour the filling evenly over the crust, gently spreading with a rubber spatula so the nuts and liquid are evenly distributed. Keep the air fryer at 176°C and cook for 12 minutes, or until mixture is bubbling. 6. Remove the pan from the air fryer and sprinkle the tart with the sea salt. Cool completely on a wire rack until room temperature. 7. Transfer the pan to the refrigerator to chill. When cold, use the foil overhang to remove the tart from the pan and cut into 8 wedges. Serve at room temperature.

Brownie Muffins

Servings: 10
Cooking Time: 15 Minutes
Ingredients:
- 2 eggs
- 96g all-purpose flour
- 1 tsp vanilla
- 130g powdered sugar
- 25g cocoa powder
- 37g pecans, chopped
- 1 tsp cinnamon
- 113g butter, melted

Directions:
1. In a bowl, whisk eggs, vanilla, butter, sugar, and cinnamon until well mixed.
2. Add cocoa powder and flour and stir until well combined.
3. Add pecans and fold well.
4. Pour batter into the silicone muffin moulds.
5. Insert a crisper plate in Ninja Foodi air fryer baskets.
6. Place muffin moulds in both baskets.
7. Select zone 1, then select "bake" mode and set the temperature to 360 degrees F for 15 minutes. Press "match" and then "start/stop" to begin.

Nutrition:
- (Per serving) Calories 210 | Fat 10.5g | Sodium 78mg | Carbs 28.7g | Fiber 1g | Sugar 20.2g | Protein 2.6g

Lemon Raspberry Muffins

Servings: 6
Cooking Time: 15 Minutes
Ingredients:
- 220 g almond flour
- 75 g powdered sweetener
- 1¼ teaspoons baking powder
- ⅓ teaspoon ground allspice
- ⅓ teaspoon ground star anise
- ½ teaspoon grated lemon zest
- ¼ teaspoon salt
- 2 eggs
- 240 ml sour cream
- 120 ml coconut oil
- 60 g raspberries

Directions:
1. Preheat the air fryer to 176ºC. Line a muffin pan with 6 paper cases.
2. In a mixing bowl, mix the almond flour, sweetener, baking powder, allspice, star anise, lemon zest, and salt.
3. In another mixing bowl, beat the eggs, sour cream, and coconut oil until well mixed. Add the egg mixture to the flour mixture and stir to combine. Mix in the raspberries.
4. Scrape the batter into the prepared muffin cups, filling each about three-quarters full.
5. Bake for 15 minutes, or until the tops are golden and a toothpick inserted in the middle comes out clean.
6. Allow the muffins to cool for 10 minutes in the muffin pan before removing and serving.

Berry Crumble And S'mores

Servings: 8
Cooking Time: 15 Minutes
Ingredients:
- Berry Crumble:
- For the Filling:
- 300 g mixed berries
- 2 tablespoons sugar
- 1 tablespoon cornflour
- 1 tablespoon fresh lemon juice
- For the Topping:
- 30 g plain flour
- 20 g rolled oats
- 1 tablespoon granulated sugar
- 2 tablespoons cold unsalted butter, cut into small cubes
- Whipped cream or ice cream (optional)
- S'mores:
- Coconut, or avocado oil, for spraying
- 8 digestive biscuits
- 2 (45 g) chocolate bars
- 4 large marshmallows

Directions:
1. Make the Berry Crumble :
2. 1. Preheat the air fryer to 204ºC. For the filling: In a round baking pan, gently mix the berries, sugar, cornflour, and lemon juice until thoroughly combined.
3. For the topping: In a small bowl, combine the flour, oats, and sugar. Stir the butter into the flour mixture until the mixture has the consistency of breadcrumbs.
4. Sprinkle the topping over the berries. 5. Put the pan in the zone 1 air fryer drawer and air fry for 15 minutes. Let cool for 5 minutes on a wire rack. 6. Serve topped with whipped cream or ice cream, if desired.
3. Make the S'mores :
4. Line the zone 2 air fryer drawer with baking paper and spray lightly with oil.
5. Place 4 biscuits into the prepared drawer.
6. Break the chocolate bars in half, and place 1/2 on top of each biscuit. Top with 1 marshmallow.
7. Air fry at 188ºC for 30 seconds, or until the marshmallows are puffed, golden brown and slightly melted.
8. Top with the remaining biscuits and serve.

Mocha Pudding Cake Vanilla Pudding Cake

Servings: 8
Cooking Time: 25 Minutes
Ingredients:
- FOR THE MOCHA PUDDING CAKE
- 1 cup all-purpose flour
- ⅔ cup granulated sugar
- 1 cup packed light brown sugar, divided
- 5 tablespoons unsweetened cocoa powder, divided
- 2 teaspoons baking powder
- ¼ teaspoon kosher salt
- ½ cup unsweetened almond milk
- 2 teaspoons vanilla extract
- 2 tablespoons vegetable oil
- 1 cup freshly brewed coffee
- FOR THE VANILLA PUDDING CAKE
- 1 cup all-purpose flour
- ⅔ cup granulated sugar, plus ½ cup
- 2 teaspoons baking powder
- ¼ teaspoon kosher salt
- ½ cup unsweetened almond milk
- 2½ teaspoons vanilla extract, divided
- 2 tablespoons vegetable oil
- ¾ cup hot water
- 2 teaspoons cornstarch

Directions:
1. To prep the mocha pudding cake: In a medium bowl, combine the flour, granulated sugar, ½ cup of brown sugar, 3 tablespoons of cocoa powder, the baking powder, and salt. Stir in the almond milk, vanilla, and oil to form a thick batter.
2. Spread the batter in the bottom of the Zone 1 basket. Sprinkle the remaining ½ cup brown sugar and 2 tablespoons of cocoa powder in an even layer over the batter. Gently pour the hot coffee over the batter (do not mix).
3. To prep the vanilla pudding cake: In a medium bowl, combine the flour, ⅔ cup of granulated sugar, the baking powder, and salt. Stir in the almond milk, 2 teaspoons of vanilla, and the oil to form a thick batter.
4. Spread the batter in the bottom of the Zone 2 basket.
5. In a small bowl, whisk together the hot water, cornstarch, and remaining ½ cup of sugar and ½ teaspoon of vanilla. Gently pour over the batter (do not mix).
6. To cook both pudding cakes: Insert both baskets in the unit.
7. Select Zone 1, select BAKE, set the temperature to 330°F, and set the timer to 25 minutes. Select MATCH COOK to match Zone 2 settings to Zone 1.
8. Press START/PAUSE to begin cooking.
9. When cooking is complete, the tops of the cakes should be dry and set.
10. Let the cakes rest for 10 minutes before serving. The pudding will thicken as it cools.

Nutrition:
- (Per serving) Calories: 531; Total fat: 8g; Saturated fat: 1g; Carbohydrates: 115g; Fiber: 3.5g; Protein: 5g; Sodium: 111mg

Fluffy Layered Peanut Butter Cheesecake Brownies

Servings: 6
Cooking Time: 35 Minutes
Ingredients:
- ½ cup blanched finely ground almond flour
- 1 cup powdered erythritol, divided
- 2 tablespoons unsweetened cocoa powder
- ½ teaspoon baking powder
- ¼ cup unsalted butter, softened
- 2 large eggs, divided
- 8 ounces full-fat cream cheese, softened
- ¼ cup heavy whipping cream
- 1 teaspoon vanilla extract
- 2 tablespoons no-sugar-added peanut butter

Directions:
1. In a large bowl, combine ½ cup erythritol, almond flour, baking powder and cocoa powder. Add in butter and one egg, stir well.
2. Spoon mixture into 6&quot| round baking pan. Put pan into the air fryer basket.
3. Set the temperature to 300°F, then set the timer for 20 minutes.
4. A toothpick inserted in center will come out clean when fully cooked. Allow to completely cool for 20 minutes and firm up.
5. In a large bowl, beat heavy cream, cream cheese, remaining ½ cup erythritol, peanut butter, remaining egg, and vanilla until turns fluffy.
6. Spoon mixture over cooled brownies. Return the pan into the air fryer basket.
7. Set the temperature to 300°F, then set the timer for 15 minutes.
8. When fully done, cheesecake will be slightly browned and mostly firm with
9. a slight jiggle. Let it rest and refrigerate for at least 2 hours before serving.

Banana Spring Rolls With Hot Fudge Dip

Servings: 4
Cooking Time: 10 Minutes
Ingredients:
- FOR THE BANANA SPRING ROLLS
- 1 large banana
- 4 egg roll wrappers
- 4 teaspoons light brown sugar
- Nonstick cooking spray
- FOR THE HOT FUDGE DIP
- ¼ cup sweetened condensed milk
- 2 tablespoons semisweet chocolate chips
- 1 tablespoon unsweetened cocoa powder
- 1 tablespoon unsalted butter
- ⅛ teaspoon kosher salt
- ⅛ teaspoon vanilla extract

Directions:
1. To prep the banana spring rolls: Peel the banana and halve it crosswise. Cut each piece in half lengthwise, for a total of 4 pieces.
2. Place one piece of banana diagonally across an egg roll wrapper. Sprinkle with 1 teaspoon of brown sugar. Fold the edges of the egg roll wrapper over the ends of the banana, then roll to enclose the banana inside. Brush the edge of the wrapper with water and press to seal. Spritz with cooking spray. Repeat with the remaining bananas, egg roll wrappers, and brown sugar.
3. To prep the hot fudge dip: In an ovenproof ramekin or bowl, combine the condensed milk, chocolate chips, cocoa powder, butter, salt, and vanilla.
4. To cook the spring rolls and hot fudge dip: Install a crisper plate in each of the two baskets. Place the banana spring rolls seam-side down in the Zone 1 basket and insert the basket in the unit. Place the ramekin in the Zone 2 basket and insert the basket in the unit.
5. Select Zone 1, select AIR FRY, set the temperature to 390°F, and set the timer to 10 minutes.
6. Select Zone 2, select BAKE, set the temperature to 330°F, and set the timer to 8 minutes. Select SMART FINISH.
7. Press START/PAUSE to begin cooking.
8. When the Zone 2 timer reads 3 minutes, press START/PAUSE. Remove the basket and stir the hot fudge until smooth. Reinsert the basket and press START/PAUSE to resume cooking.
9. When cooking is complete, the spring rolls should be crisp.
10. Let the hot fudge cool for 2 to 3 minutes. Serve the banana spring rolls with hot fudge for dipping.

Nutrition:
- (Per serving) Calories: 268; Total fat: 10g; Saturated fat: 4g; Carbohydrates: 42g; Fiber: 2g; Protein: 5g; Sodium: 245mg

Baked Apples

Servings: 4
Cooking Time: 20 Minutes
Ingredients:
- 4 granny smith apples, halved and cored
- ¼ cup old-fashioned oats (not the instant kind)
- 1 tablespoon butter, melted
- 2 tablespoon brown sugar
- ½ teaspoon ground cinnamon
- Whipped cream, for topping (optional)

Directions:
1. Insert the crisper plates into the drawers. Lay the cored apple halves in a single layer into each of the drawers. Insert the drawers into the unit.
2. Select zone 1, select AIR FRY, set temperature to 350°F, and set time to 10 minutes. Select MATCH to match zone 2 settings to zone 1. Press the START/STOP button to begin cooking.
3. Meanwhile, mix the oats, melted butter, brown sugar, and cinnamon to form the topping.
4. Add the topping to the apple halves when they've cooked for 10 minutes.
5. Select zone 1, select BAKE, set temperature to 390°F, and set time to 22 minutes. Select MATCH to match zone 2 settings to zone 1. Press the START/STOP button to begin cooking.
6. Serve warm and enjoy!

Soft Pecan Brownies

Servings: 6
Cooking Time: 20 Minutes
Ingredients:
- ½ cup blanched finely ground almond flour
- ½ cup powdered erythritol
- 2 tablespoons unsweetened cocoa powder
- ½ teaspoon baking powder
- ¼ cup unsalted butter, softened
- 1 large egg
- ¼ cup chopped pecans
- ¼ cup low-carb, sugar-free chocolate chips

Directions:
1. Stir erythritol, almond flour, baking powder and cocoa powder in a large bowl. Add in egg and butter, mix well.
2. Fold in chocolate chips and pecans. Pour mixture into 6&quot| round baking pan. Put pan into the air fryer basket.
3. Set the temperature to 300°F, then set the timer for 20 minutes.
4. A toothpick inserted in center will come out clean when completely cooked. Let it rest for 20 minutes to fully cool and firm up. Serve immediately.

Air Fried Bananas

Servings: 4
Cooking Time: 15 Minutes
Ingredients:
- 4 bananas, sliced
- 1 avocado oil cooking spray

Directions:
1. Spread the banana slices in the two crisper plates in a single layer.
2. Drizzle avocado oil over the banana slices.
3. Return the crisper plate to the Ninja Foodi Dual Zone Air Fryer.
4. Choose the Air Fry mode for Zone 1 and set the temperature to 350 degrees F and the time to 13 minutes.
5. Select the "MATCH" button to copy the settings for Zone 2.
6. Initiate cooking by pressing the START/STOP button.
7. Serve.

Pumpkin-spice Bread Pudding

Servings: 6
Cooking Time: 35 Minutes
Ingredients:
- Bread Pudding:
- 175 ml heavy whipping cream
- 120 g canned pumpkin
- 80 ml whole milk
- 65 g granulated sugar
- 1 large egg plus 1 yolk
- ½ teaspoon pumpkin pie spice
- ⅛ teaspoon kosher, or coarse sea salt
- 1/3 loaf of day-old baguette or crusty country bread, cubed
- 4 tablespoons unsalted butter, melted
- Sauce:
- 80 ml pure maple syrup
- 1 tablespoon unsalted butter
- 120 ml heavy whipping cream
- ½ teaspoon pure vanilla extract

Directions:
1. For the bread pudding: In a medium bowl, combine the cream, pumpkin, milk, sugar, egg and yolk, pumpkin pie spice, and salt. Whisk until well combined.
2. In a large bowl, toss the bread cubes with the melted butter. Add the pumpkin mixture and gently toss until the ingredients are well combined. 3. Transfer the mixture to a baking pan. Place the pan in the zone 1 air fryer drawer. Set the temperature to 176°C cooking for 35 minutes, or until custard is set in the middle. 4. Meanwhile, for the sauce: In a small saucepan, combine the syrup and butter. Heat over medium heat, stirring, until the butter melts. Stir in the cream and simmer, stirring often, until the sauce has thickened, about 15 minutes. Stir in the vanilla. Remove the pudding from the air fryer. 5. Let the pudding stand for 10 minutes before serving with the warm sauce.

Grilled Peaches

Servings: 4
Cooking Time: 10 Minutes
Ingredients:
- 2 yellow peaches
- ¼ cup graham cracker crumbs
- ¼ cup brown sugar
- ¼ cup butter, diced into tiny cubes
- Whipped cream or ice cream, for serving.

Directions:
1. Cut the peaches into wedges and pull out their pits.
2. Install a crisper plate in both drawers. Put half of the peach wedges into the drawer in zone 1 and half in zone 2's. Sprinkle the tops of the wedges with the crumbs, sugar, and butter. Insert the drawers into the unit.
3. Select zone 1, select AIR FRY, set the temperature to 390°F, and set the time to 10 minutes. Select MATCH to match zone 2 settings to zone 1. Press the START/STOP button to begin cooking.

Pecan Brownies And Cinnamon-sugar Almonds

Servings: 10
Cooking Time: 20 Minutes
Ingredients:
- Pecan Brownies:
- 50 g blanched finely ground almond flour
- 55 g powdered sweetener
- 2 tablespoons unsweetened cocoa powder
- ½ teaspoon baking powder
- 55 g unsalted butter, softened
- 1 large egg
- 35 g chopped pecans
- 40 g low-carb, sugar-free chocolate chips
- Cinnamon-Sugar Almonds:
- 150 g whole almonds
- 2 tablespoons salted butter, melted
- 1 tablespoon granulated sugar
- ½ teaspoon ground cinnamon

Directions:
1. Make the Pecan Brownies :
2. In a large bowl, mix almond flour, sweetener, cocoa powder, and baking powder. Stir in butter and egg.
3. Fold in pecans and chocolate chips. Scoop mixture into a round baking pan. Place pan into the zone 1 air fryer basket.
4. Adjust the temperature to 150°C and bake for 20 minutes.
5. When fully cooked a toothpick inserted in center will come out clean. Allow 20 minutes to fully cool and firm up.
6. Make the Cinnamon-Sugar Almonds :
7. In a medium bowl, combine the almonds, butter, sugar, and cinnamon. Mix well to ensure all the almonds are coated with the spiced butter.
8. Transfer the almonds to the zone 2 air fryer basket and shake so they are in a single layer. Set the air fryer to 150°C, and cook for 8 minutes, stirring the almonds halfway through the cooking time.
9. Let cool completely before serving.

Easy Mini Chocolate Chip Pan Cookie

Servings: 4
Cooking Time: 7 Minutes
Ingredients:
- ½ cup blanched finely ground almond flour
- ¼ cup powdered erythritol
- 2 tablespoons unsalted butter, softened
- 1 large egg
- ½ teaspoon unflavored gelatin
- ½ teaspoon baking powder
- ½ teaspoon vanilla extract
- 2 tablespoons low-carb, sugar-free chocolate chips

Directions:
1. Combine erythritol and almond flour in a large bowl. Add in egg, gelatin, and butter , stir well.
2. Stir in vanilla and baking powder and then fold in chocolate chips. Spoon batter into 6&quot| round baking pan. Put pan into the air fryer basket.
3. Set the temperature to 300°F, then set the timer for 7 minutes.
4. The top of the cookie will be golden brown and a toothpick inserted in center will come out clean when fully cooked. Allow to rest for more than 10 minutes.

Bread Pudding

Servings: 2
Cooking Time: 15 Minutes
Ingredients:
- Nonstick spray, for greasing ramekins
- 2 slices of white bread, crumbled
- 4 tablespoons white sugar
- 5 large eggs
- ½ cup cream
- Salt, pinch
- ⅓ teaspoon cinnamon powder

Directions:
1. Take a bowl and whisk eggs in it.
2. Add sugar and salt to the eggs and whisk it all well.
3. Then add cream and use a hand beater to incorporate the Ingredients:.
4. Next add cinnamon, and the crumbled white bread.
5. Mix it well and add into two round shaped baking pans.
6. Place each baking pan in the air fryer basket.
7. Set zone 1 to AIR FRY mode at 350 degrees F for 8-12 minutes.
8. Press MATCH button for zone 2.
9. Once it's cooked, serve.

Snacks And Appetizers Recipes

Fried Halloumi Cheese

Servings: 6
Cooking Time: 12 Minutes.
Ingredients:
- 1 block of halloumi cheese, sliced
- 2 teaspoons olive oil

Directions:
1. Divide the halloumi cheese slices in the crisper plate.
2. Drizzle olive oil over the cheese slices.
3. Return the crisper plate to the Ninja Foodi Dual Zone Air Fryer.
4. Choose the Air Fry mode for Zone 1 and set the temperature to 360 degrees F and the time to 12 minutes.
5. Flip the cheese slices once cooked halfway through.
6. Serve.

Nutrition:
- (Per serving) Calories 186 | Fat 3g | Sodium 223mg | Carbs 31g | Fiber 8.7g | Sugar 5.5g | Protein 9.7g

Bacon Wrapped Tater Tots

Servings: 8
Cooking Time: 15 Minutes
Ingredients:
- 8 bacon slices
- 3 tablespoons honey
- ½ tablespoon chipotle chile powder
- 16 frozen tater tots

Directions:
1. Cut the bacon slices in half and wrap each tater tot with a bacon slice.
2. Brush the bacon with honey and drizzle chipotle chile powder over them.
3. Insert a toothpick to seal the bacon.
4. Place the wrapped tots in the air fryer baskets.
5. Return the air fryer basket 1 to Zone 1, and basket 2 to Zone 2 of the Ninja Foodi 2-Basket Air Fryer.
6. Choose the "Air Fry" mode for Zone 1 at 350 degrees F and 14 minutes of cooking time.
7. Select the "MATCH COOK" option to copy the settings for Zone 2.
8. Initiate cooking by pressing the START/PAUSE BUTTON.
9. Serve warm.

Chicken Stuffed Mushrooms

Servings: 6
Cooking Time: 15 Minutes.
Ingredients:
- 6 large fresh mushrooms, stems removed
- Stuffing:
- ½ cup chicken meat, cubed
- 1 (4 ounces) package cream cheese, softened
- ¼ lb. imitation crabmeat, flaked
- 1 cup butter
- 1 garlic clove, peeled and minced
- Black pepper and salt to taste
- Garlic powder to taste
- Crushed red pepper to taste

Directions:
1. Melt and heat butter in a skillet over medium heat.
2. Add chicken and sauté for 5 minutes.
3. Add in all the remaining ingredients for the stuffing.
4. Cook for 5 minutes, then turn off the heat.
5. Allow the mixture to cool. Stuff each mushroom with a tablespoon of this mixture.
6. Divide the stuffed mushrooms in the two crisper plates.
7. Return the crisper plate to the Ninja Foodi Dual Zone Air Fryer.
8. Choose the Air Fry mode for Zone 1 and set the temperature to 375 degrees F and the time to 15 minutes.
9. Select the "MATCH" button to copy the settings for Zone 2.
10. Initiate cooking by pressing the START/STOP button.
11. Serve warm.

Nutrition:
- (Per serving) Calories 180 | Fat 3.2g | Sodium 133mg | Carbs 32g | Fiber 1.1g | Sugar 1.8g | Protein 9g

Onion Pakoras

Servings: 2
Cooking Time: 10 Minutes
Ingredients:
- 2 medium brown or white onions, sliced (475 ml)
- 120 ml chopped fresh coriander
- 2 tablespoons vegetable oil
- 1 tablespoon chickpea flour
- 1 tablespoon rice flour, or 2 tablespoons chickpea flour
- 1 teaspoon ground turmeric
- 1 teaspoon cumin seeds
- 1 teaspoon rock salt
- ½ teaspoon cayenne pepper
- Vegetable oil spray

Directions:
1. In a large bowl, combine the onions, coriander, oil, chickpea flour, rice flour, turmeric, cumin seeds, salt, and cayenne. Stir to combine. Cover and let stand for 30 minutes or up to overnight. Mix well before using.
2. Spray the air fryer baskets generously with vegetable oil spray. Drop the batter in 6 heaping tablespoons into the two baskets. Set the air fryer to 175°C for 8 minutes. Carefully turn the pakoras over and spray with oil spray. Set the air fryer for 2 minutes, or until the batter is cooked through and crisp, checking at 6 minutes for doneness. Serve hot.

Fried Pickles

Servings: 4
Cooking Time: 15 Minutes
Ingredients:
- 2 cups sliced dill pickles
- 1 cup flour
- 1 tablespoon garlic powder
- 1 tablespoon Cajun spice
- ½ tablespoon cayenne pepper
- Olive Oil or cooking spray

Directions:
1. Mix together the flour and spices in a bowl.
2. Coat the sliced pickles with the flour mixture.
3. Place a crisper plate in each drawer. Put the pickles in a single layer in each drawer. Insert the drawers into the unit.
4. Select zone 1, then AIR FRY, then set the temperature to 400 degrees F/ 200 degrees C with a 15-minute timer. To match zone 2 settings to zone 1, choose MATCH. To begin, select START/STOP.

Nutrition:
- (Per serving) Calories 161 | Fat 4.1g | Sodium 975mg | Carbs 27.5g | Fiber 2.2g | Sugar 1.5g | Protein 4g

Parmesan French Fries

Servings: 6
Cooking Time: 20 Minutes.
Ingredients:
- 3 medium russet potatoes
- 2 tablespoons parmesan cheese
- 2 tablespoons fresh parsley, chopped
- 1 tablespoon olive oil
- Salt, to taste

Directions:
1. Wash the potatoes and pass them through the fries' cutter to get ¼-inch-thick fries.
2. Place the fries in a colander and drizzle salt on top.
3. Leave these fries for 10 minutes, then rinse.
4. Toss the potatoes with parmesan cheese, oil, salt, and parsley in a bowl.
5. Divide the potatoes into the two crisper plates.
6. Return the crisper plates to the Ninja Foodi Dual Zone Air Fryer.
7. Choose the Air Fry mode for Zone 1 and set the temperature to 360 degrees F and the time to 20 minutes.
8. Select the "MATCH" button to copy the settings for Zone 2.
9. Initiate cooking by pressing the START/STOP button.
10. Toss the chips once cooked halfway through, then resume cooking.
11. Serve warm.

Nutrition:
- (Per serving) Calories 307 | Fat 8.6g |Sodium 510mg | Carbs 22.2g | Fiber 1.4g | Sugar 13g | Protein 33.6g

Cinnamon Sugar Chickpeas

Servings: 4
Cooking Time: 15 Minutes
Ingredients:
- 2 cups chickpeas, drained
- Spray oil
- 1 tablespoon coconut sugar
- ½ teaspoon cinnamon
- Serving
- 57g cheddar cheese, cubed
- ¼ cup raw almonds
- 85g jerky, sliced

Directions:
1. Toss chickpeas with coconut sugar, cinnamon and oil in a bowl.
2. Divide the chickpeas into the Ninja Foodi 2 Baskets Air Fryer baskets.
3. Drizzle cheddar cheese, almonds and jerky on top.
4. Return the air fryer basket 1 to Zone 1, and basket 2 to Zone 2 of the Ninja Foodi 2-Basket Air Fryer.
5. Choose the "Air Fry" mode for Zone 1 at 380 degrees F and 15 minutes of cooking time.
6. Select the "MATCH COOK" option to copy the settings for Zone 2.
7. Initiate cooking by pressing the START/PAUSE BUTTON.
8. Toss the chickpeas once cooked halfway through.
9. Serve warm.

Tofu Veggie Meatballs

Servings: 4
Cooking Time: 15 Minutes
Ingredients:
- 122g firm tofu, drained
- 50g breadcrumbs
- 37g bamboo shoots, thinly sliced
- 22g carrots, shredded & steamed
- 1 tsp garlic powder
- 1 ½ tbsp soy sauce
- 2 tbsp cornstarch
- 3 dried shitake mushrooms, soaked & chopped
- Pepper
- Salt

Directions:
1. Add tofu and remaining ingredients into the food processor and process until well combined.
2. Insert a crisper plate in the Ninja Foodi air fryer baskets.
3. Make small balls from the tofu mixture and place them in both baskets.
4. Select zone 1, then select "air fry" mode and set the temperature to 380 degrees F for 10 minutes. Press "match" to match zone 2 settings to zone 1. Press "start/stop" to begin. Turn halfway through.

Tangy Fried Pickle Spears

Servings: 6
Cooking Time: 15 Minutes
Ingredients:
- 2 jars sweet and sour pickle spears, patted dry
- 2 medium-sized eggs
- 80 ml milk
- 1 teaspoon garlic powder
- 1 teaspoon sea salt
- ½ teaspoon shallot powder
- ⅓ teaspoon chilli powder
- 80 ml plain flour
- Cooking spray

Directions:
1. Preheat the air fryer to 195°C. Spritz the zone 1 air fryer basket with cooking spray.
2. In a bowl, beat together the eggs with milk. In another bowl, combine garlic powder, sea salt, shallot powder, chilli powder and plain flour until well blended.
3. One by one, roll the pickle spears in the powder mixture, then dredge them in the egg mixture. Dip them in the powder mixture a second time for additional coating.
4. Arrange the coated pickles in the prepared basket. Air fry for 15 minutes until golden and crispy, shaking the basket halfway through to ensure even cooking.
5. Transfer to a plate and let cool for 5 minutes before serving.

Kale Potato Nuggets

Servings: 4
Cooking Time: 15 Minutes
Ingredients:
- 279g potatoes, chopped, boiled & mashed
- 268g kale, chopped
- 1 garlic clove, minced
- 30ml milk
- Pepper
- Salt

Directions:
1. In a bowl, mix potatoes, kale, milk, garlic, pepper, and salt until well combined.
2. Insert a crisper plate in the Ninja Foodi air fryer baskets.
3. Make small balls from the potato mixture and place them both baskets.
4. Select zone 1 then select "air fry" mode and set the temperature to 390 degrees F for 15 minutes. Press "match" to match zone 2 settings to zone 1. Press "start/stop" to begin. Turn halfway through.

Mozzarella Arancini

Servings: 16 Arancini
Cooking Time: 8 To 11 Minutes
Ingredients:
- 475 ml cooked rice, cooled
- 2 eggs, beaten
- 355 ml panko breadcrumbs, divided
- 120 ml grated Parmesan cheese
- 2 tablespoons minced fresh basil
- 16 ¾-inch cubes Mozzarella cheese
- 2 tablespoons olive oil

Directions:
1. Preheat the air fryer to 205°C.
2. In a medium bowl, combine the rice, eggs, 120 ml of the breadcrumbs, Parmesan cheese, and basil. Form this mixture into 16 1½-inch balls.
3. Poke a hole in each of the balls with your finger and insert a Mozzarella cube. Form the rice mixture firmly around the cheese.
4. On a shallow plate, combine the remaining 240 ml of the breadcrumbs with the olive oil and mix well. Roll the rice balls in the breadcrumbs to coat.
5. Air fry the arancini in two baskets for 8 to 11 minutes or until golden brown.
6. Serve hot.

Crab Cakes

Servings: 4
Cooking Time: 15 Minutes
Ingredients:
- 227g lump crab meat
- 1 red capsicum, chopped
- 3 green onions, chopped
- 3 tablespoons mayonnaise
- 3 tablespoons breadcrumbs
- 2 teaspoons old bay seasoning
- 1 teaspoon lemon juice

Directions:
1. Mix crab meat with capsicum, onions and the rest of the ingredients in a food processor.
2. Make 4 inch crab cakes out of this mixture.
3. Divide the crab cakes into the Ninja Foodi 2 Baskets Air Fryer baskets.
4. Return the air fryer basket 1 to Zone 1, and basket 2 to Zone 2 of the Ninja Foodi 2-Basket Air Fryer.
5. Choose the "Air Fry" mode for Zone 1 at 370 degrees F and 10 minutes of cooking time.
6. Select the "MATCH COOK" option to copy the settings for Zone 2.
7. Initiate cooking by pressing the START/PAUSE BUTTON.
8. Flip the crab cakes once cooked halfway through.
9. Serve warm.

Fried Ravioli

Servings: 6
Cooking Time: 10 Minutes
Ingredients:
- 12 frozen raviolis
- 118ml buttermilk
- ½ cup Italian breadcrumbs

Directions:
1. Dip the ravioli in the buttermilk then coat with the breadcrumbs.
2. Divide the ravioli into the Ninja Foodi 2 Baskets Air Fryer baskets.
3. Return the air fryer basket 1 to Zone 1, and basket 2 to Zone 2 of the Ninja Foodi 2-Basket Air Fryer.
4. Choose the "Air Fry" mode for Zone 1 and set the temperature to 400 degrees F and 7 minutes of cooking time.
5. Select the "MATCH COOK" option to copy the settings for Zone 2.
6. Initiate cooking by pressing the START/PAUSE BUTTON.
7. Flip the ravioli once cooked halfway through.
8. Serve warm.

Bacon-wrapped Shrimp And Jalapeño

Servings: 8
Cooking Time: 26 Minutes
Ingredients:
- 24 large shrimp, peeled and deveined, about 340 g
- 5 tablespoons barbecue sauce, divided
- 12 strips bacon, cut in half
- 24 small pickled jalapeño slices

Directions:
1. Toss together the shrimp and 3 tablespoons of the barbecue sauce. Let stand for 15 minutes. Soak 24 wooden toothpicks in water for 10 minutes. Wrap 1 piece bacon around the shrimp and jalapeño slice, then secure with a toothpick.
2. Preheat the air fryer to 175°C.
3. Place the shrimp in the two air fryer baskets, spacing them ½ inch apart. Air fry for 10 minutes. Turn shrimp over with tongs and air fry for 3 minutes more, or until bacon is golden brown and shrimp are cooked through.
4. Brush with the remaining barbecue sauce and serve.

Cheese Stuffed Mushrooms

Servings: 4
Cooking Time: 10 Minutes
Ingredients:
- 176g button mushrooms, clean & cut stems
- 46g sour cream
- 17g cream cheese, softened
- ½ tsp garlic powder
- 58g cheddar cheese, shredded
- Pepper
- Salt

Directions:
1. In a small bowl, mix cream cheese, garlic powder, sour cream, pepper, and salt.
2. Stuff cream cheese mixture into each mushroom and top each with cheddar cheese.
3. Insert a crisper plate in the Ninja Foodi air fryer baskets.
4. Place the stuffed mushrooms in both baskets.
5. Select zone 1 then select "air fry" mode and set the temperature to 370 degrees F for 8 minutes. Press "match" to match zone 2 settings to zone 1. Press "start/stop" to begin.

Caramelized Onion Dip With White Cheese

Servings: 8 To 10
Cooking Time: 30 Minutes
Ingredients:
- 1 tablespoon butter
- 1 medium onion, halved and thinly sliced
- ¼ teaspoon rock salt, plus additional for seasoning
- 113 g soft white cheese
- 120 ml sour cream
- ¼ teaspoon onion powder
- 1 tablespoon chopped fresh chives
- Black pepper, to taste
- Thick-cut potato crisps or vegetable crisps

Directions:
1. Place the butter in a baking pan. Place the pan in the zone 1 air fryer basket. Set the air fryer to 90°C for 1 minute, or until the butter is melted. Add the onions and salt to the pan.
2. Set the air fryer to 90°C for 15 minutes, or until onions are softened. Set the air fryer to 190°C for 15 minutes, until onions are a deep golden brown, stirring two or three times during the cooking time. Let cool completely.
3. In a medium bowl, stir together the cooked onions, soft white cheese, sour cream, onion powder, and chives. Season with salt and pepper. Cover and refrigerate for 2 hours to allow the flavours to blend.
4. Serve the dip with potato crisps or vegetable crisps.

Bruschetta With Basil Pesto

Servings: 4
Cooking Time: 5 To 11 Minutes
Ingredients:
- 8 slices French bread, ½ inch thick
- 2 tablespoons softened butter
- 240 ml shredded Mozzarella cheese
- 120 ml basil pesto
- 240 ml chopped grape tomatoes
- 2 spring onions, thinly sliced

Directions:
1. Preheat the air fryer to 175°C.
2. Spread the bread with the butter and place butter-side up in the two air fryer baskets. Bake for 3 to 5 minutes, or until the bread is light golden brown.
3. Remove the bread from the baskets and top each piece with some of the cheese. Return to the baskets in 2 baskets and bake for 1 to 3 minutes, or until the cheese melts.
4. Meanwhile, combine the pesto, tomatoes, and spring onions in a small bowl.
5. When the cheese has melted, remove the bread from the air fryer and place on a serving plate. Top each slice with some of the pesto mixture and serve.

Crispy Filo Artichoke Triangles

Servings: 18 Triangles
Cooking Time: 9 To 12 Minutes
Ingredients:
- 60 ml Ricotta cheese
- 1 egg white
- 80 ml minced and drained artichoke hearts
- 3 tablespoons grated Mozzarella cheese
- ½ teaspoon dried thyme
- 6 sheets frozen filo pastry, thawed
- 2 tablespoons melted butter

Directions:
1. Preheat the air fryer to 205°C.
2. In a small bowl, combine the Ricotta cheese, egg white, artichoke hearts, Mozzarella cheese, and thyme, and mix well.
3. Cover the filo pastry with a damp kitchen towel while you work so it doesn't dry out. Using one sheet at a time, place on the work surface and cut into thirds lengthwise.
4. Put about 1½ teaspoons of the filling on each strip at the base. Fold the bottom right-hand tip of phyllo over the filling to meet the other side in a triangle, then continue folding in a triangle. Brush each triangle with butter to seal the edges. Repeat with the remaining phyllo dough and filling.
5. Place the triangles in the two air fryer baskets. Bake, 6 at a time, in two baskets for about 3 to 4 minutes, or until the filo is golden brown and crisp.
6. Serve hot.

"fried" Ravioli With Zesty Marinara

Servings: 6
Cooking Time: 20 Minutes
Ingredients:
- FOR THE RAVIOLI
- ¼ cup all-purpose flour
- 1 large egg
- 1 tablespoon water
- ⅔ cup Italian-style bread crumbs
- 1 pound frozen cheese ravioli, thawed
- Nonstick cooking spray
- FOR THE MARINARA
- 1 (28-ounce) can chunky crushed tomatoes with basil and oregano
- 1 tablespoon unsalted butter
- 2 garlic cloves, minced
- ¼ teaspoon kosher salt
- ¼ teaspoon red pepper flakes

Directions:
1. To prep the ravioli: Set up a breading station with three small shallow bowls. Put the flour in the first bowl. In the second bowl, beat the egg and water. Place the bread crumbs in the third bowl.
2. Bread the ravioli in this order: First dip them into the flour, coating both sides. Then dip into the beaten egg. Finally, coat them in the bread crumbs, gently pressing the crumbs into the ravioli to help them stick.
3. Mist both sides of the ravioli generously with cooking spray.
4. To prep the marinara: In the Zone 2 basket, combine the crushed tomatoes, butter, garlic, salt, and red pepper flakes.
5. To cook the ravioli and sauce: Install a crisper plate in the Zone 1 basket and add the ravioli to the basket. Insert the basket in the unit. Insert the Zone 2 basket in the unit.
6. Select Zone 1, select AIR FRY, set the temperature to 390°F, and set the time to 20 minutes.
7. Select Zone 2, select BAKE, set the temperature to 350°F, and set the time to 15 minutes. Select SMART FINISH.
8. Press START/PAUSE to begin cooking.
9. When the Zone 1 timer reads 7 minutes, press START/PAUSE. Remove the basket and shake to redistribute the ravioli. Reinsert the basket and press START/PAUSE to resume cooking.
10. When cooking is complete, the breading will be crisp and golden brown. Transfer the ravioli to a plate and the marinara to a bowl. Serve hot.

Nutrition:
- (Per serving) Calories: 282; Total fat: 8g; Saturated fat: 3g; Carbohydrates: 39g; Fiber: 4.5g; Protein: 13g; Sodium: 369mg

RECIPES INDEX

A

Acorn Squash Slices 75

Air Fried Bananas 92

Air Fryer Sausage Patties 18

Air-fried Tofu Cutlets With Cacio E Pepe Brussels Sprouts 80

Air-fried Turkey Breast With Roasted Green Bean Casserole 60

Almond Chicken 66

Asian Pork Skewers 48

Asparagus And Bell Pepper Strata And Greek Bagels 24

B

Bacon Cheese Egg With Avocado And Potato Nuggets 17

Bacon Wrapped Pork Tenderloin 53

Bacon Wrapped Tater Tots 94

Bacon-wrapped Chicken 61

Bacon-wrapped Filet Mignon 57

Bacon-wrapped Shrimp 28

Bacon-wrapped Shrimp And Jalapeño 98

Baked Apples 91

Baked Mushroom And Mozzarella Frittata With Breakfast Potatoes 21

Balsamic Duck Breast 64

Banana Bread 20

Banana Spring Rolls With Hot Fudge Dip 91

Bang Bang Shrimp With Roasted Bok Choy 28

Bang-bang Chicken 70

Barbecue Ribs With Roasted Green Beans And Shallots 51

Basil Cheese S·saltalmon 33

Basil Cheese Salmon 30

Bbq Corn 82

Bbq Pork Chops 44

Bbq Pork Spare Ribs 58

Beef Kofta Kebab 57

Beef Ribs Ii 57

Berry Crumble And S'mores 89

Blackened Red Snapper 39

Brazilian Chicken Drumsticks 69

Bread Pudding 93

Breaded Summer Squash 79

Breakfast Meatballs 26

Breakfast Potatoes 23

Breakfast Sausage Omelet 16

Breakfast Stuffed Peppers 26

Broiled Crab Cakes With Hush Puppies 37

Brownie Muffins 89

Bruschetta With Basil Pesto 98

Brussels Sprouts 76

Buffalo Bites 78

Butter-wine Baked Salmon 32

C

Canadian Bacon Muffin Sandwiches And All-in-one Toast 23

Caprese Panini With Zucchini Chips 77

Caramelized Fruit Skewers 87

Caramelized Onion Dip With White Cheese 98

Cheddar-stuffed Chicken 70

Cheese Stuffed Mushrooms 98

Cheeseburgers With Barbecue Potato Chips 45

Chicken & Veggies 72

Chicken And Potatoes 62

Chicken And Vegetable Fajitas 60

Chicken Bites 59

Chicken Breast Strips 66

Chicken Parmesan 70

Chicken Patties And One-dish Chicken Rice 71

Chicken Potatoes 74

Chicken Shawarma 71

Chicken Stuffed Mushrooms 94

Chicken Thighs In Waffles 63

Chickpea Fritters 81

Chili Honey Salmon 27

Chinese Bbq Pork 55

Chipotle Drumsticks 61

Chocolate Chip Cake 86

Churros 87

Cinnamon Air Fryer Apples 25

Cinnamon Apple French Toast 12

Cinnamon Rolls 19

Cinnamon Sugar Chickpeas 96

Cinnamon Toasts 13

Cinnamon-apple Pork Chops 58

Cinnamon-raisin Bagels Everything Bagels 22

Citrus Mousse 83

Classic Fish Sticks With Tartar Sauce 37

Cod With Jalapeño 32

Cornish Hen 73

Cornish Hen With Asparagus 63

Country Prawns 40

Crab Cakes 97

Cracked-pepper Chicken Wings 75

Crispy Dill Chicken Strips 66

Crispy Filo Artichoke Triangles 99

Crusted Chicken Breast 68

Crustless Prawn Quiche 38

Curried Orange Honey Chicken 72

D

Donuts 22

Dukkah-crusted Halibut 35

E

Easy Breaded Pork Chops 49

Easy Mini Chocolate Chip Pan Cookie 93

Easy Pancake Doughnuts 18

Egg And Avocado In The Ninja Foodi 16

Egg And Bacon Muffins 20

Egg In Bread Hole 14

Egg White Muffins 14

Eggs In Avocado Cups 17

F

Fajita Chicken Strips & Barbecued Chicken With Creamy Coleslaw 65

Falafel 78

Fish Sandwich 42

Five-spice Pork Belly 46

Flavourful Mexican Cauliflower 75

Fluffy Layered Peanut Butter Cheesecake Brownies 90

Fried Asparagus 76

Fried Halloumi Cheese 94

Fried Lobster Tails 33

Fried Olives 79

Fried Pickles 95

Fried Prawns 27

Fried Ravioli 97

Fried Tilapia 36

Frozen Breaded Fish Fillet 38

Fruity Blackberry Crisp 82

G

Garlic Butter Steak Bites 50

Garlic Butter Steaks 45

Glazed Steak Recipe 46

Glazed Thighs With French Fries 67

Gluten-free Spice Cookies 86

Gochujang Brisket 55

Greek Chicken Meatballs 62

Greek Chicken Souvlaki 61

Green Beans With Baked Potatoes 78

Grilled Peaches 92

Gyro Breakfast Patties With Tzatziki 18

H

Ham Burger Patties 52

Healthy Air Fried Veggies 77

Herbed Prawns Pita 39

Honey Banana Oatmeal 16

Honey Butter Chicken 59

Honey Pecan Shrimp 29

Honey-glazed Chicken Thighs 62

J

Jerk-rubbed Pork Loin With Carrots And Sage 43

K

Kale And Spinach Chips 76

Kale Potato Nuggets 97

Keto Baked Salmon With Pesto 30

Kielbasa Sausage With Pineapple And Kheema Meatloaf 48

L

Lamb Shank With Mushroom Sauce 56

Lemon Pepper Fish Fillets 34

Lemon Raspberry Muffins 89

Lemon-pepper Chicken Thighs With Buttery Roasted Radishes 69

Lime Glazed Tofu 76

M

Maple-pecan Tart With Sea Salt 88

Marinated Salmon Fillets 41

Meat And Rice Stuffed Peppers 44

Meatballs 51

Meatloaf 53

Miso Salmon And Oyster Po'boy 29

Mocha Pudding Cake Vanilla Pudding Cake 90

Moist Chocolate Espresso Muffins 85

Mongolian Beef With Sweet Chili Brussels Sprouts 50

Monkey Bread 86

Morning Patties 24

Mozzarella Arancini 97

Mozzarella Bacon Calzones 14

N

New York Strip Steak 47

Nutty Granola 12

Nutty Prawns With Amaretto Glaze 41

O

Onion Pakoras 95

Orange-mustard Glazed Salmon 33

P

Panko-crusted Fish Sticks 36

Parmesan French Fries 95

Parmesan Ranch Risotto And Oat And Chia Porridge 25

Parmesan-crusted Fish Sticks With Baked Macaroni And Cheese 31

Pecan Brownies And Cinnamon-sugar Almonds 93

Pecan-crusted Chicken Tenders 73

Pepper Egg Cups 15

Pepper Poppers 79

Perfect Parmesan Salmon 35

Pineapple Wontons 84

Pork Chops With Apples 46

Potato And Parsnip Latkes With Baked Apples 81

Prawn Creole Casserole And Garlic Lemon Scallops 32

Puff Pastry 25

Pumpkin French Toast Casserole With Sweet And Spicy Twisted Bacon 26

Pumpkin Hand Pies Blueberry Hand Pies 83

Pumpkin-spice Bread Pudding 92

Q

Quiche Breakfast Peppers 20

R

Rainbow Salmon Kebabs And Tuna Melt 30

Roast Beef With Yorkshire Pudding 47

Roasted Beef 53

Roasted Garlic Chicken Pizza With Cauliflower "wings" 67

Roasted Salmon Fillets & Chilli Lime Prawns 38

Rosemary And Garlic Lamb Chops 54

Rosemary Ribeye Steaks And Mongolian-style Beef 54

S

Salmon With Broccoli And Cheese 40

Sausage & Bacon Omelet 13

Sausage & Butternut Squash 17

Sausage And Cauliflower Arancini 43

Sausage And Cheese Balls 15

Sausage And Egg Breakfast Burrito 15

Savory Salmon Fillets 36

Sesame Ginger Chicken 64

Simply Terrific Turkey Meatballs 59

Soft Pecan Brownies 92

Speedy Chocolate Espresso Mini Cheesecake 87

Spicy Chicken 72

Spicy Chicken Sandwiches With "fried" Pickles 74

Spicy Lamb Chops 51

Spinach Egg Muffins 12

Steak And Asparagus Bundles 42

Steak In Air Fry 49

Steamed Cod With Garlic And Swiss Chard 39

Stuffed Mushrooms With Crab 41

Sumptuous Pizza Tortilla Rolls 44

Sweet And Spicy Country-style Ribs 52

Sweet Potato Donut Holes 82

Sweet Potatoes & Brussels Sprouts 80

Sweet Protein Powder Doughnut Holes 84

T

Taco Seasoned Steak 52

Tandoori Prawns 35

Tangy Fried Pickle Spears 96

Teriyaki Chicken Skewers 73

Thai Prawn Skewers And Lemon-tarragon Fish En Papillote 34

Tofu Veggie Meatballs 96

Tomahawk Steak 56

Tuna With Herbs 40

Tuna-stuffed Quinoa Patties 27

Turkey And Beef Meatballs 49

Two-way Salmon 31

V

Vanilla Strawberry Doughnuts 21

Victoria Sponge Cake 85

W

Walnuts Fritters 88

Whole Chicken 65

Wholemeal Banana-walnut Bread 13

Wholemeal Blueberry Muffins 19

Wings With Corn On The Cob 64

Y

Yellow Potatoes With Eggs 19

Yogurt Lamb Chops 58

Z

Zesty Cranberry Scones 84

Printed in Great Britain
by Amazon